THE FLYING LIFE

stories for the aviation soul

BY THE SAME AUTHOR

If Airplanes Could Talk: The Pilot's Book of Wit and Wisdom

Man Things: Equal Time for Men

THE FLYING LIFE

stories for the aviation soul

Lauran Paine Jr.

CASCADE PUBLISHING

SALEM, OREGON

Portions of *The Flying Life: stories for the aviation soul* originally appeared, in somewhat different form, in *Sport Aviation* and *Pilot Getaways*.

© 2010 by Lauran Paine Jr.

Printed in the United States of America.

Published by Cascade Publishing
Salem, Oregon 97304

Paine, Lauran, Jr.
   The flying life: stories for the aviation soul
Private flying - Anecdotes, facetiae, satire, etc./Lauran Paine Jr. - 1st ed.

ISBN: 978-0-9657607-0-6

for my bride of forty-one years who has,
often in person and always in spirit,
been with me for every takeoff and landing

CONTENTS

INTRODUCTION

This book is a direct result of the encouragement of others. It is a compilation of my articles published in the pages of Experimental Aviation Association's *Sport Aviation* magazine as well as *Pilot Getaways* magazine, and a few from earlier writings, including my airline newsletter. It has been my pleasure to write for these publications over the past ten years. My motivation to compile the articles into book form came from readers who share my passion and love for aviation and who responded that they enjoyed reading them.

I began writing about aviation, not because I thought I could write, but because I like to share stories. The literary journey has given back much more than I could have imagined in the form of friends, good friends, who have encouraged and inspired me. They have given me much more to write about than my own experiences. There is a connection between those who fly, build or dream airplanes.

Some of the articles included in this book are my favorites and many more, from what you've told me, are yours. Combined they make a book. For your support, for the knowledge you've shared and for the flying life, I am forever thankful.

Lauran Paine, Jr.

1

TEACHING YOUR SON TO FLY

That's him in the front seat of the airplane, learning to fly. I'm in the back seat and we're on the downwind. That's not the back of just any head in front of me. That's my son.

So many thoughts racing through my mind: remembering when he was born, watched and listened as those first halting breaths turned that blue little body pink. Held him. Tears. Got him a fishing pole that first day. Used to push him in his stroller and pull him in his wagon. He used to ride in the 'kiddie-seat' on the back of my bicycle.

Then the journey to independence began, that is still unfolding today: his first tricycle, yellow with white spoke wheels. Stenciled on the back of the seat was "World Champion Ankle Biter Bull Rider." The two-wheeler: I remember running behind it, pushing and steadying, until that day he rode off alone. The handlebars were gyrating wildly, but he was upright and moving under his own power.

On to cars: the fence post that caught the open side passenger door as he was backing up; the light bumping of his buddy's car at the stoplight because he thought it would be funny and the cop who didn't think it was funny; the minor fender-bender at a residential street intersection when he called and asked, "What do I do, Dad?" And I answered, "Handle it!" Tough love. Tough to say that when for all the years when he fell I ran to pick him up. My parental doubts were later allayed when he told me, "Dad, I needed you to say that."

Then the day came, "Dad, I want to learn how to fly." It was something I had neither encouraged nor discouraged. His Mom reminded me, "That's my baby, you know."

How to go about it? I bought an Aeronca Champ, circa 1946. Just wings, tail, tail wheel, stick, rudder, oil pressure and airspeed. To us she was a thing of beauty. I made him change the oil. Lying on his back, oil running down his hands and dripping off his elbow, I asked him, "Is this fun?" I got an unequivocal, "Yeah, this is great!"

The flying: what a joy! He took to it like a duck to water. Soaked it all up like a sponge. I worried I might be missing something; I haven't done much light airplane instructing. I'm a bit hazy on some of the airspace structure and cloud clearance requirements, but he wasn't. He read the books and watched the videos, then refreshed me. But I knew the basic airmanship I wanted to get across: respect for the machine, awareness and courtesy in the air, look before you turn, hard work and study, recognizing limits, respecting weather, being on-speed to land (tail draggers have a way of teaching that all by themselves).

The whole scene was a joy. Riding to the airport, talking with our hands. Lunches with the good ol' boys at the local airport café, "How's that boy doin'?" I could honestly answer, "Fine!" The glow after the flights, the satisfaction of progression, the excited conversation pursuant to a goal being accomplished-- it was all there.

As we progressed, I watched the mechanics of flight come to him. The day came for pattern work. Once again I became a spectator to my son's journey, "Let's take this thing around the patch. Handle it!" He never hesitated. He'd taxi out, swing around to take a look at the pattern and line up on the runway. The power came up, the tail lifted and the mains came off the ground and, before I knew it, he was on the downwind...where this story began. And the memories flowed. There could have been a public airshow that day and I wouldn't have paid any attention. My son was flying.

Opposite the touch down point, the power came back. I hoped he remembered the carb heat. I knew he would, but dads worry like that. Base to final, the sound of an airplane in glide, the nose came up gently, the tail touched, then the mains. The Champ rolled straight, the rudder wiggling, the power came up and he was on his way again, and again, and again. I know the feeling. He was lost in joy. I finally looked away after a bit to take in the moment. I'm supposed to be a crusty ol' dad. It must have been the light breeze that made my eyes water. He had mastered yet another journey.

He was leaving for college soon, but the ride home from the airport that day was one to remember. His head was high, his eyes bright, his smile huge and his excitement contagious, "Dad, I got off the centerline a little on the fourth one." It was my chance for some dad-philosophy, "That's okay. What matters is that you're always trying to get back on." Then, "Son, I'm proud of you."

The excitement continued at home as he told all to his mom. I went to get cleaned up for dinner. When I came back to the kitchen, he was still telling his mom.

What's next? Don't know. College graduation? Marriage? Family? More flying? Whatever. The choices are his. I just want him to be happy and productive. And this day he was. It's a memory I'll cherish forever.

2

BEGINNINGS

When did it happen to you? The first time—that moment—when you knew that aviation was something special, that it would be a part of your life, one way or another, forever. We don't often think of such things; sometimes they are a little fuzzy in our memory or even unknown. Sometimes they are clear and when we think about them they make us smile. They were the beginning of something that is good in our lives.

Every life has conception, every bonfire a spark, every thing an initial idea, and every aviation career (and it is a career, whether you're getting paid for it or not) a beginning. In sharing what I think my moment was, see if you can pick it out. Then share yours with me, and we'll both smile. Smiles are good. I like smiles. And at EAA we have lots of them. I like that, too.

The meadow was a magical place. I didn't realize it at the time, but it was. I did know that it was my boy-place. It lay between our house and the barn. It had hills on one side and a river on the other. It was a broad expanse of various types of grass with clover and cow-pies mixed in. Both of the latter were OK. The clover was cause for hunting the elusive four-leaf versions and it was the cows that kept the meadow mowed. Each had its rights.

The meadow was magical because only good things happened there, and it was there that I always found happiness. I could be a running back carrying a football, dodging cow-pie tackles with adroit moves, tripping myself and falling down, and getting up again slowly with great courage to the roar of the crowd that was the hill and the river. Second down. Tackled again. Always, always getting back up. I could do that all day. Touching the barn was a touchdown, and I touched it a lot.

When the game was over I could be a gymnast and run and tumble and handspring and tumble some more to the wind's roar of approval. Or I could throw a baseball in the air, hit it with the bat, and watch it soar into the blue. The wall I hit it over was always just in front of wherever the ball landed. "Another home run!" I would say to myself as I trotted around the cow-pie bases.

I was never alone on the meadow. I had my imagination, my spirit, and Brucie, my big ol' gentle, tail-wagging, tongue-hanging-out, smiling, always there, always happy Collie dog. When I was in football-land he would run beside me and, until the next down, would sit by the line of scrimmage when I got "tackled." In baseball-land Brucie was key—he retrieved the balls I would throw up and hit. After about the 10th home run, he would get the ball (he always got it), but on the return trip he'd veer off about halfway back, plop down, drop the ball between his feet, and look at me. It was time for the seventh inning stretch.

The seventh inning stretch was great. Going to Brucie, I'd lay down and rest my head on his flank, and we'd talk and dream. Sometimes we'd just watch the puffy white clouds float by. If it was 2:10 p.m., from horizon to horizon we'd watch a lone Douglas DC-3 drone overhead, the deep-throated rumble of its radial engines striking a chord in my heart.

Sometimes I think I may have gone to sleep in the peace. Brucie must have, too, because he never moved until I did. What a friend he was—never complained, never criticized, always listened, and was always fun. No one ever had to explain to me what friendship was. Brucie had already taught me. He was a big part of the meadow's magic.

Sometimes my dad would put me on the tractor on the meadow, a Ford model 8N. And I do mean "put me on it." He'd just set me on the seat, put the tractor in the lowest gear (I couldn't reach the pedals but I could steer), get it going, then he would get off and I would steer all over the meadow. Child cruelty? Hardly. I loved it.

Behind the tractor was a heavy screen. I'd drag it around and break up the cow-pies. Wherever they were, and they were everywhere, that is where I steered. It helped to fertilize the field by "spreading the wealth," so to speak. When my dad figured the field was finished he'd walk alongside the tractor, swing up on it, and push in the clutch. When it stopped I would get off with a great feeling of accomplishment and head for whatever was next. I still love tractors, especially Ford 8Ns.

The meadow had bees and butterflies and gnats and ants. I spent a lot of time marveling at what it was they did, so industrious and purposeful. That is a good way to be. I never wondered why they did what they did. It didn't seem to matter. That they were doing it was good enough for me. And that they did it so well was almost motivational. No, it was motivational. Nature's a good example of how to live.

Through all this the two milk cows kept their peace and their place on the meadow. Green grass makes good milk. They would munch, lie down, and chew their cud. They shared the meadow nicely. That is what made it so great. It was a beautiful place and we all shared it equally and nicely.

That is what the world needs, more meadows and less graffiti. Every kid should have a meadow where he or she can go and be "alone," be safe, dream—and just be. A meadow is a great start on life.

Did you spot my aviation moment? Was it anything like yours? Whatever yours was, I'll bet it's kinda special to think about, isn't it? Go with it. Bask in its goodness. Aviation has been good to me: It gave me dreams to dream and it now gives me perspective from above. Not to mention the wonderful people I have met along the way. And I love to share it. Like Brucie did. I still have a picture of him on my desk.

3

MAKING A DIFFERENCE

Do you remember the people who made a difference in your life? I'm not talking about parents, teachers, heroes, and the like. I'm talking about chance meetings, incidents, people whose names you don't remember. But what they did for you is seared in your memory—what they said, what they did, and what they shared. Moments to remember. Magic moments. Given to you by someone who cared and asked no favor. They gave just to give. In an aviation career, those people are legion.

When I was about 7 years old, my mom took me to an "air show" at the local airport, where a few airplanes were on static display. We drove up and parked in the gravel parking lot. And there they sat—airplanes. There for me to look at. With their doors open. And people standing beside them who smiled.

There was a jet there, too. The sign said it was a T-33. It was silver and shiny and there was a guy in a neat flying suit, complete with patches and stuff, standing by it. I stood by the T-33, in awe. Kicking the dirt and pushing my hands into my pockets, I was stealing glances at the jet when the Cool Guy with all the patches said, "Come over here, son." Me? You, Cool Guy, talking to me??!!? I looked around and there was no one else standing there. Just me. I took a few steps forward and Cool Guy did the same. When I was in range he picked me up and stood me on the wing of that T-33. On the wing! Me! Then he pointed to the cockpit and said, "Take a look."

I leaned over the canopy rail and looked inside. Yow! There were enough dials and switches in there to keep a boy busy and happy for a lifetime. In that moment, Cool Guy made a difference in my life. I ended up flying in the Air Force and flew single-pilot in the National Guard for 16 years. Single-pilot fighter flying remains my favorite. Those young military days are over for me now, but I am building

Van's RV-8, and it'll be silver and shiny with a stick grip from a T-33. I don't know where Cool Guy is today, but he gave me something special. I hope that somewhere in his heart, he knows.

Then there was Mr. Gregory. (In the 1950s, all adult males were "mister.") A friend of the family, he did something for a living but I don't know what it was. I do know that he traveled a lot and stopped by only occasionally. And he was taking flying lessons. He took me with him one day when he went to the airport for a lesson. I watched him and his instructor walk around the little yellow airplane. They called it a J-3. Mr. Gregory climbed in, as did his instructor. A guy spun the prop around and the engine started. It was an awesome sound, a rhythmic idle with the sound of wind thrown in. It was a symphony to my ears, even though I didn't know what a symphony was. I watched Mr. Gregory take off.

Prop Spinner Guy watched me watch Mr. Gregory take off. Then he said, "C'mon over here and you can sit in this airplane while you're waiting. This airplane's called a Champ." I climbed in. I didn't want to touch anything, but I did grab hold of the stick. I moved it ever so carefully. Something out on the wings moved. Cool! I pulled the stick back and I couldn't see anything move. But it must move something, I reasoned. Looking behind me, I pulled on the stick and something on the tail moved. Wow! I was moving things out there from in here. How cool is that?

Every once in a while Prop Spinner Guy would peek out of the hangar, look at me, and smile. I sat in the Champ until Mr. Gregory came back. I liked being there. As we drove home that day I don't remember saying much. I was just thinking in that boyish-dreaming sort of way. Mr. Gregory said, "Airplanes are kinda neat, huh?"

All I said was, "Yup." But I was feeling a lot more than just "yup." I've owned a Champ, and am in negotiations for another. Every time I see one, my head turns. Why? Mr. Gregory and Prop Spinner Guy, that's why.

I must have been 10 or 11 years old when I got sick. Not serious sick, just "kid sick." Stomach, or something like that. I didn't know it then (but I do now) that parents don't like to see their kids sick. So my dad said, "When you get well, we'll go for an airplane ride." It would be my first! A bolt of resolve shot through me. Instead of sickness getting me down, I resolved to get the sickness down. I willed myself well. (It's still good to be able to do that; of course, it helps to be young.)

Three days later, we were at the airport. My Dad had bought us tickets from Montague, California to Medford, Oregon and back. When the DC-3 taxied up my heart must have kept beating, but those deep throated, clanking engines made me breathless. Then the engines stopped, it became quiet, and I started breathing again.

The door in the back opened and the stewardess waved. I figured she noticed me because I was really dressed up; my Mom made me wear a shirt that had a collar and had to be ironed. She motioned us over and we got in. Up the aisle we went and I sat about mid-wing, next to the right engine. The airplane smelled good. I don't know what it was, but it just smelled really good.

When the engines started I was one with them, with their noise and vibration. Then the airplane moved, rocking over the pavement until it swung around and got really loud. The scenery started changing fast and the ground fell away—and I was flying, flying, flying. That's all my mind was saying— "I'm flying, flying, flying."

Magic. Scenery. Goodness. There's the hill my brother and I built a fort on. It was a clear day, with just a few clouds. The airplane bounced along over the Siskiyou Mountains, rocking and bumping and flexing. The wings flexed and a little oil seeped from around the engine cowling. The mechanical stuff was cool, too. My Dad just sort of sat, looked over at me more than he looked outside. He didn't seem that enamored with it, but a promise is a promise. (It still is.)

We landed in Medford, got out, and stood on the ramp while men fueled the airplane for the return trip. A guy with some stripes on his sleeve came up, patted me on the shoulder, and said, "How ya doin', son?" I didn't answer. I was too awestruck to say any words. I just looked up at him and smiled a wide-eyed smile. He knew I was doin' just fine.

My Dad said, "That's the captain." My boy-mind flashed with the thought, "Wow, pilot's are regular people, too." I felt everything again on the return trip. Eighteen years later, I flew a DC-3 in Korea and once ferried one from Korea to Japan to Okinawa to Guam to Wake to Midway to Hawaii. And what I felt when I was 10 or 11, 1 felt it all again. The DC-3 was a history-maker. My first flight was in it; I'm glad I got to fly it. And thanks for the moment, Captain.

The first time I took the controls of an airplane I was probably twelve years old. Some "people from San Francisco," as my parents called them, flew up to look at our ranch. It was for sale. That was the

19

first time I knew ranching had anything to do with money. Up to then it had been working the cows, mowing and raking hay, hauling bales, chopping weeds along the irrigation ditches, riding horses, fishing, and harvesting the garden.

One of the guys from San Francisco had an airplane. Somebody said he was a doctor. Being a doctor didn't mean much to me; I'd never been to one. But having an airplane did. The doctor sensed something from me, so while sale negotiations were taking place—that meant three men leaning on a fence, chewing on pieces of straw, glancing at the scenery a lot, and talking a little— he asked if I wanted to go for a ride. My smile and my eyes said yes. I asked if I could bring my best buddy, Ozzie, along. The doctor said, "Sure." Soon we three were at the airport.

The doctor called the airplane an Apache. He started it and taxied while I held the door part way open to keep the breeze coming in the cockpit. I felt the power of the wind and I liked it. Then we closed the door and took off. We circled the ranch. He told me to take hold of the yoke. I did, with both hands. "Turn the yoke to the left," doctor said. "Now to the right." Then, "Now make it go where you want it to go."

Was I hooked? What do you think?

That was 43 years ago and I'm still turning left and right and, when I'm in my own airplane, going where I want to go. Ozzie later got his private pilot certificate. That afternoon, the doctor made a difference; he helped spawn a passion. I think he knew: His eyes sparkled when he smiled at me.

There are people like those you've met in your aviation life, too, aren't there? Not necessarily with names, but with memorable, difference-making moments. You gotta love 'em. I do.

And to those of you today who are giving, be it at the local airport, a school, in a hangar, at a chance meeting, or at an EAA Young Eagle's rally, you're making special moments. You may not know it, or what comes of it, but you're the catalyst for something special. And I know why you are doing it: Because somebody gave to you. You are merely giving back. There is precious little in life that is better than giving.

I can't close without saying to Cool Guy, to Mr. Gregory and Prop Spinner Guy, to Captain, and to doctor, "For sharing with a small boy, in your own way, the magic of flight, thank you."

4

OLD DOG, NEW TRICKS

Does building an airplane make you a better pilot? I have reason to think so. I'm not saying that building an airplane will make you a good pilot; I'm saying that if you are already a pretty darn good pilot, building an airplane will make you a better one.

Why?

Because you learn so much. You learn about the construction process, the engineering process, the planning, the thinking, yourself, and about the energy and sheer dedication that go into making an airplane. In other words, you gain not just knowledge but an appreciation for the airplane you fly. And that makes you a better pilot.

I wouldn't have said all this until a couple years ago, and I've been flying for more than 30 years. But then, at the invitation of my son, who brought an ad to my attention, I went to the mountain and saw the light. I went to Van's Aircraft in North Plains, Oregon. I live in Salem, Oregon, so the journey wasn't a long one, which made the decision easier. Besides, my teenage son said he'd buy breakfast, and that is an event that doesn't happen very often (as you who have teenage children know full well).

Arriving in North Plains, we "hang a right" (I'm riding with my teenage son, remember?) at an intersection. There aren't very many intersections in North Plains—three, maybe four, tops. One-half block and there it sat—a large, older, unassuming, virtually unmarked metal building. There was one sign, faded, that said "Van's Aircraft."

We were in the right place.

Outside were a few parked vehicles, mostly pickups. Pickups outside is a good sign that there are real people inside (as opposed to "beautiful people"). In the front of the building is a red door, also faded. That must be where you go in—we deduced that because it was the only door, not because it said "Entrance" or anything like that. It didn't. We tried the faded red door. It opened with a squeak and a swipe and we went in. I liked the door. I know, silly me. But I just happen to like function more than I like image.

Inside, I wasn't disappointed. The "foyer" was small. Okay, tiny. It was like a short hallway with a counter on one side. This was a no-nonsense place. Here you push, pull, buy something, or get out of the way. It was an airplane place. Pure and simple. I liked it. I liked it a lot. It didn't seem to matter that my blue jeans were a little (okay, a lot) faded or that my T-shirt had a small hole by my right shoulder. That wouldn't cut it at Smith-Barney, but it was just fine at Van's. Of course, I was feeling pretty good to begin with because my stomach was full and my son paid for it. (You have to be the parent of a teenager to really understand what I'm saying.)

A lady behind one of the two desks looked up after hanging up the phone—which rang again immediately after she'd hung up. The lady at the other desk answered it. Lady number one asked, "May I help you?"

"We'd like to see some information on the RV-8, maybe walk around the factory, something like that," we said. Under the Plexiglas on the counter was a note: "Please call ahead for tours or when picking up parts." Oops, noticed that a little late, didn't we? But the nice lady said, "Sure. I'll see what I can do."

My son and I stood in the foyer with our hands in our pockets, looking at the pictures—all RV's—and the grease pencil board labeled "Kit Lead Times."

Then out came a tall, lanky, mustachioed, friendly man with a steady eye and a firm handshake, "Hi, I'm Tom Greene. Let's step out in the shop."

Out into the shop we go and— wow—what an ambience. Airplane parts everywhere. Piled high. Bent pieces of aluminum. Landing gear. Bins of rivets. Canopies. Wooden shipping boxes. You could stand in the middle of the building, do a three-sixty, and everywhere you looked was great stuff. None of it pretentious. All of it functional. What can I say? A place like that just warms your heart. And it smelled good. How does it smell good? I can't explain it. It just does.

A few people scurried about here and there amid the . . . not clutter, uh, let's just call it "organized mayhem." Tom Greene had a word—actually, a lot of words—for every scurrying person. And every one of them had several words back for him. Factory banter. It was, as my son put it, "Way cool."

Out we went to the back building, all the while answering Tom's new-acquaintance-type questions like, "What do you do?"

A lot of places I take that question to mean, "How much money do you have?" I didn't take it that way here, for this was a place of passion and where there is passion, money be damned. Hey, if I scooped dog poop for a living, I'd still figure a way to get enough money to buy an RV-8. The darn thing is that sexy.

In the back building—machines. Machines that bend aluminum. Machines that cut. Machines that drill holes, lots of holes at once. And beside the machines are piles of parts, ready to go to building number one.

That is the cycle: from aluminum sheets, to parts, to stockpiles, to sales, to me. Or you. And from there to the magnificent journey of self-discovery that is building an airplane. The bug bit me—the I want to build an airplane bug—and bit bad. But first we had to go home; I'd forgotten the checkbook. On the way, we stopped for lunch (I bought). We discussed that we didn't have to decide "if," only "when."

Two weeks later, after matching mutual days off (and calling ahead), my son and I were back at Van's. This time Bill Benedict met us, an unassuming yet confident man. We drove to the airport. Actually, it was a grass strip. Grass strip sounds better than airport, doesn't it? We strapped in and Bill flew us, first me and then my son. Canopy, stick, tandem seats, tailwheel—it just doesn't get any better than that. And with the aileron touch of a fighter. Light. Responsive. Fast. Take me back to the factory and load up my truck with parts. I'm ready.

Back at the factory (we had our checkbook this time) they loaded us up with the tail kit and off we went, with a bunch of aluminum parts rattling around in the back, waiting for us to lay our hands on them. Excited? Very. Realizing a dream is exciting. And scary. "Can I?" you ask yourself. Yup. "Will I?" Yup, again. Two "yups" were all I needed to hear myself say. I was good to go.

At home, clear a space in the garage (which means, my car out, my wife's car in) and lay out the parts. Then attach the horizontal stabilizer skin to the rear spar and, presto, you have an airplane part. Wow! Easy.

Of course, later you have take the skin off the spar and final drill the holes, debur, dimple, countersink, Cleco, measure, sand, rivet—big rivets and little rivets— with your new compressor and rivet gun. All of which brings me back to my original point: the learning curve begins; the appreciation for what goes into building an airplane begins.

Now, when I preflight my airliner, guess what? I look at rivets, at skin fit, at, well, everything with a new eye. I appreciate how it's built. I look at the quality of the construction. Okay, I'll tell everybody right now, all the rivets on my RV are not perfect. So it was with great satisfaction that I found some rivets on my airliner that weren't perfect either. They were in the baggage compartment, back under a part of the fuselage that leads to the wing. They weren't bad, just not perfect. They were in a hard-to-get-to place, which is usually where my less than perfect rivets are, too. But they were still holding tight, and on the airliner they probably had a jillion or two cycles on them. I like knowing something about the details of an airplane. I didn't always, but I do now.

Besides all of the above, building an airplane is fun. I'm not setting any time lines to finish—that is key for me. I'm just going to enjoy every piece, every rivet, every accomplishment, overcome every frustration, and press on—someday it will all be an airplane. And when I fly it I'll know it better than any airplane I've ever flown. I'm going to like that feeling.

In the meanwhile, it's helping me to know and appreciate the airliner I fly. I like that, too. Will it do the same for you? I don't know. But I do know that it can't hurt and, besides, you get to meet a lot of nice people in the process.

Aviation is a journey of many paths. The path I've just described is one of learning, accomplishment, joy, and good people. Try it. You'll like it.

5

HANGIN' OUT WITH BUMS

You don't hear about them much any more. In today's hustle and bustle world they may have gotten a bad name, so people don't talk about being related to one. But airport bums are still out there; it's just that they keep to themselves, in a clannish sort of way. They are the strong, silent type—except that when they are among their own kind, you can't shut them up.

Many airport bums have other lives. They are teachers, businessmen, physicians, and truck drivers, but they are bums nonetheless. Among them are some interesting characters. To visit them you have to go to their natural habitat—the local airport.

The local airport is just that—local. And small. One runway. Away from town, a local airport has ambience, one small building—the FBO, with gas pumps out back. There might be a chain-link fence between the gravel parking lot and the FBO, just three feet high and without barbed wire. There's no gate. The cracking concrete sidewalk, with some bright yellow daffodils growing beside it, passes through an opening in the fence.

The door squeaks when you go into the building. The counter is a display case that has some logbooks, manuals, and E6B computers (the manual type) for sale on the shelves under its glass top. The prices are handwritten on little stickers—no bar coding here. There are a few tables—hey, a sandwich shop! I'll bet the bums gather here regularly, around noon. We'll come back then. For now, let's just nod "howdy" and walk on through to the hangars.

Hangars are the airport bum's habitat. Walk slowly. Move slowly. Nothing happens fast here. There are many hangars, but no motif. Just rectangular buildings. Wood. Aluminum. Steel. Some painted, some not. Some have doors. Some don't. If there are doors and they're cracked open, there is someone inside. Usually, you start on the ones without doors.

You spot one! An airport bum in his natural setting. Your first glimpse is usually just a torso. His head is inside or under something, like a cowling or fuselage. Your first words don't startle a bum. In their world invitations are open; open area equals open invitation.

Bums seldom stop what they're doing when they speak, they just say "howdy" and keep working. When they finish what they're doing they'll come out and look at you. In the eye. Like a real person. In a real conversation. None of the "have a nice day" stuff. Names aren't an issue. It's where you are, not who you are. Names come later. "Howzit going?" you ask.

"Fine. Just tryin' to fix this framitz. I put a new one on 10 years ago. Darn things don't hold up like they should ... well, it wasn't new when I put it on. It was up on a shelf down at Joe's hangar. You know Joe. (Everybody knows everybody here, or is supposed to.) He said, 'Take it.' So I did. Guess I can't complain about the price, huh? But I'll get it fixed. Got all week to do it. Heck, I'll get another 10 years out of it. And if it goes haywire again, I'll complain about how it didn't hold up. Hey, you got a minute? Mind goin' down to Joe's hangar? He's in there. I need to borrow his framitz-remover. No need buyin' one long as I can borrow his. If he gives you any lip, tell him I'll buy his lunch. He knows I won't, but he likes to hear it anyway."

See? I told you that in their habitat you can't shut them up. And he dang well knows I have a minute. You don't hang around airport hangars unless you have a lot of minutes. "Sure. I'll go down there for you."

"Hey, what's your name?"

"Lauran."

"Warren?"

"No. Lauran, with an L."

"Nice to meet you, Warren. I'm Pete." We shake hands. Pete's hands are a little dirty, but that's OK. Here, what kind of clothes you wear and whether your hands are dirty have nothing to do with anything.

As we wander down to Joe's hangar, let me tell you about Pete. He flew 100 missions in P-51s in Korea. I could listen to him talk all day about the power, the speed, the sound, the feel, and the fears he felt in that airplane. He loved the Mustang—"Ol' 99" he calls it. (That was its tail number.) He's proud he served. Not boastful. And I'm proud just to hang out with him.

Joe's in his hangar, with his head wedged between a Stearman's heat shield and its Lycoming's cylinders. "Pete asked if he could borrow the framitz remover." No need for chitchat or formalities here. Say what you have to say and do what you have to do.

"Yeah. It's over by that old mag on the table. Did he say he'd buy my lunch?"

"Sure did."

"You tell him I said he's a lying sack of sheep dung."

"OK. I'll be sure and pass that on." On the table by the old mag ("old" being a relative term because it looks like it's been untouched in 20 years) is the framitz remover. Grabbing it, I head out the door, and Joe's head comes out. Balding, he has a big grease spot high on his forehead. His hands are black with grime. "I gotta get Kyle to look at this widget with me," he says. "Some of these young kids don't get much hands-on around these old airplanes. He's a great kid, though. Always willing to help." Kyle is the FBO's young mechanic. Then Joe reminds me, "Don't forget to tell Pete what I told ya."

"I'll be sure and tell him." Joe is a physician. You'd never know it, talking to him. Someone would have to tell you. All Joe talks about is airplanes.

Back at Pete's, "Here's the framitz remover." The torso bent over the cowling says, "Thanks. Put it over by that Cub carcass. This guy rebuilt it, painted it with dope, and was hauling it to the airport when he flicked a cigarette out his pickup window and caught the dang Cub on fire. Asked if he could dump it in the corner. Said he'd be back later, but that was a year ago. Ain't seen him since. That's about right. Takes about a year for something like that to wear off. Hey, Joe say something about me being a sack of something-or-other?"

"Uh, yeah. Matter of fact, he did."

"I'd buy his dang lunch someday, but he'd have a heart attack if I did, and I'm not sure the next guy would let me borrow the framitz remover." A hearty laugh reverberates under the cowling.

I tell Pete, "I gotta go down to Mary's hangar. Told her I'd help her with the new wheel bearings."

"She sure takes good care of that airplane."

"Yeah, she does. You going to the sandwich shop later?"

"Maybe." Pete always goes to the sandwich shop. It's a ritual, but he has to keep 'em guessing. "Nice meetin' ya, Warren."

At Mary's, the 172 is older, with a straight back, straight tail. But it is spiffy. Clean as a whistle, it gleams with pride. Mary's kneeling by the right main gear, its wheel off. She greets me with, "About got it done. Bearing was bad. Pete says they don't hold up like they used to. See what you think."

I look, knowing that Mary knows a lot more about this airplane than I do, and say, "Looks good to me. Nice job."

"I'll have Kyle check it this afternoon." Mary teaches third grade. Loves her kids. Loves her airplane. It's a good combination; she's a good person. To Mary, NOW means immediately, not National Organization for Women. NABO (National Airport Bum Organization) is the only organization she really cares about, and she's a member in very good standing. (Bums are unisex, much to the chagrin of the politically correct crowd.)

It's lunchtime and they're all at the sandwich shop—Pete, Joe, Mary, John, Bud, Bill, and others whose names you don't always know but whose voices are heard. None of them look at the menu. They order the same thing day in and day out. Sometimes one of them branches out and has the special, but only when they're really feeling wild and crazy. The banter flows in a symphony of Americana, composed by character, passion, and friendship. I take it all in with pleasure. It's grass-roots aviation. Long may it last.

Pete doesn't buy Joe's lunch, and 90 minutes later they all meander back to the hangars, still bantering. I'm tellin' ya, it don't hardly get any better than a day at the local airport.

Okay, I didn't write this from afar. I wrote it from experience. I am an airport bum. To put it in perspective, let me improve on what a French philosopher once said with, "I'm an airport bum. Therefore I am.

6

REVERSE ENGINEERING

So there I was, renewing my CFI certificate online. There are sixteen lessons, about an hour each to approximate a sit-down sixteen hour weekend renewal course. There's lots of good stuff to review: aerodynamics, practical test standards, FAR's, weather, sport pilot, maneuvers, publications, GPS. And FITS. FITS? That's what I said. It's Flight Industry Training Standards.

FITS, they say, happened because current training focuses on "stick-and-rudder" skills while the majority of accidents result from lack of awareness and poor aeronautical decision making. And since the Feds are "here to help" they are now addressing the issue with FITS. It fits. (Sorry....I couldn't help myself.)

All of the above is well and good. But there's nothing wrong with focusing on stick-and-rudder skills. Most accidents, after all, occur during the landing phase of flight, when stick-and-rudder skills are all important. That said, aeronautical decision making is all important, too, as a means of keeping us on the straight-and-narrow and out of trouble. But it was how they go about teaching it that caused me to pause: the cavalcade of acronyms pouring from their cubicles was a bit much.

They use SBT (Scenario Based Training) to teach decision making skills, i.e., "You're flying at 8,500 feet. The mountain in front of you is 10,500 feet. What are you going to do?" That's all well and good, too. Then comes PAVE, a checklist to perceive hazards by evaluating the Pilot, Aircraft, enVironment and External....pressures. Then you process the hazards by CARE: Consequence, Alternatives, Reality and External pressure, again. Then you perform risk management by using TEAM: Transfer, Eliminate, Accept, and Mitigate. And to go with all this there are colorful graphics with arrows pointing to Perceive, Process, Perform, also known as the three P's.

And yet more graphics with colors and arrows pointing to Identify, Assess, Analyze, Make decisions, Use controls, Monitor results. And there is a 'likelihood scale,' a 'severity scale' and a very colorful 'risk assessment matrix.' Yikes! The idea to address decision making is a good one but cluttering it so with acronyms and pretty charts, while great for a classroom presentation, makes it rather ineffectual in a cockpit.

I can tell you from years of personal experience, from giving and receiving hundreds of check rides, when the "stuff" hits the fan it is the simplest procedures that work the best. I've seen it over and over. The complex procedures, i.e., isolating electrical buses to see where smoke is coming from (now eliminated from most airline checklists) usually are not performed well and can actually cause more problems than they solve. Pilots who know their limits will go to them...then stop. And when a problem develops they will revert to the simplest procedures, the basics, and land. No acronyms (except, maybe, GUMP). That off my chest, here's my contribution to FITS: "If you think it might hurt you, don't do it."

Now that I've "dumbed" that down, let me go the rest of the way out on my limb and tell you how I "dumbed down" my homebuilt airplane. Think of it this way: know how, when you buy a new computer, you get a lot of programs you don't use? Airplanes are sometimes like that, too. Until you build your own. Then you get to design and build your own instrument panel, exactly the way you want it, putting stuff where you want it. And, ahhhhhh, it's great fun! There is so much available out there, so many bells-and-whistles. It's intoxicating. Or not. I chose "or not."

Let me pause a minute and give you some background so you won't write to give the phone number of a good psychiatrist you know. I grew up on a farm, driving two-cylinder John Deere and four cylinder Ford tractors (one of which I still have and am restoring). I like simple. I crave simple, actually. So never mind the psychiatrist's number. And it's not like I haven't flown some pretty technologically-nifty airplanes: I flew professionally for forty years, from jet transports to single pilot military to the new "Barbie"......glass cockpit....jets. I flew the schedules and accomplished the mission....unless I thought it might hurt me (or my passengers). But now...but NOW...I fly for fun. Not for utility or because I have to be somewhere. For fun. Period. And that's why I built my airplane the way I did.

My cockpit is round-dial VFR simple. I watched a hundred people look at my instrument panel at AirVenture/Oshkosh last summer. They'd lean over, look in, look left, look right, look down, and look back up. Then their eyebrows would rise. Then they'd turn to whoever was with them and I could read their lips from a hundred yards away as they'd say, "No GPS!"

Okay, I "dumbed down" my airplane. I "reverse engineered" it for safety. How? No attitude indicator (I've never owned an airplane with one, didn't want to start now) so I am never tempted to go in or near a cloud or towards reduced visibility. That wouldn't be prudent, would it? Or lights. I don't fly it at night. Or autopilot. I actually fly the airplane the whole flight. Or VOR. Or GPS. I fly with a chart and look outside. In fact, my head's outside the cockpit about 95% of the time. No pretty little moving map with moving 'thingys' all over the place to tempt me inside. My cockpit motto is: "If it ain't required, don't put it in." And I don't go near those uppity airports that have huge circles and wedges and veils on the chart to go with the big splotches of yellow near an airport that has a zillion runways. You won't see me "on top," either. But you will see me out where the UNICOM's are.

People look at my instrument panel and ask "What are the two red-guarded switches on the right side of the panel?" That's my armament panel: one switch is labeled "guns" and the other is labeled "bombs." And they are in large part responsible for their being no enemy fighters in the skies over Oregon.

After reading all this you probably still feel like you need to call that psychiatrist, right? Don't. I've got a great family, friends (most as goofy as I), fly for fun, have an old tractor, watch football and smile a lot. Ain't nothin' else to want.

7

WHERE TO BUILD AN AIRPLANE?

(This was written pre-9/11. How times change.)

Where to build an airplane? Why, obviously, the garage. Or the basement. Or the barn. Or, for the lucky ones, in a hangar. But, truth be known, there are a lot of other places to build an airplane. Like *everywhere.*

The skin stiffeners for the rudder on my RV-8? I made those in Room 2019 at a Sacramento, California, motel. The stiffeners for the elevator? Smoothed and deburred them in Kalispell, Montana. The doublers for the rear wing spar? Worked on 'em in Calgary, Canada. Wing tie-down brackets? Measured and clamped those in Boise, Idaho.

Okay, I'm an airline pilot and travel a lot, and when I know I'll have a long layover, I take airplane parts with me. Angle. Snips. Deburring tool. Marking pens. Rulers. Clamps. Stuff like that. You see, when I'm in a motel room I refuse to watch daytime TV, and my airplane parts allow me to take a little bit of home—my shop—with me when I travel. They put me in my happy place, just like being in my shop does at home.

I'm not alone in this. I read a story about a Navy pilot who took a bunch of RV parts on a cruise with him. Six months later, he got off the boat (sorry...ship) with some ailerons, elevators, flaps, and a rudder. Completed. At sea. Good for him. I don't know what kind of daytime TV the Navy has, but I'm sure building parts for your own airplane beats it. And it's probably great stress relief from pounding a jet on a pitching wet carrier deck at night.

Construction plans are something else I take with me. I read them during deadhead flights and while waiting for flights. That way, when I get ready to work on a part, I've thought it through before I lay hands on it. That helps me a lot. Those dreaded fuel tanks with that icky Pro-Seal? I've already built them 27 times in my mind. I ain't afraid of no Pro-Seal and no fuel tanks. (In my mind, anyway—I'll let you know how the real thing turns out.)

I take my Orndorff construction videos with me, too, and watch them in motel rooms that have VCRs. It's great to have the visuals to go along with the plans. When I want to watch a tape just for pleasure, I watch Van's "The RV Story." It's delightful and inspiring.

Back to building. The wing ribs? Here's what you do: bring a bunch of them in the family room. Pull out the breadboard and put it on the floor in front of the couch, over by the fireplace. Then sit on the floor by the breadboard, resting your back on the front of the couch. Take your fluting pliers and flute the ribs straight, using the flat breadboard to check them—while watching the football game. During a time-out or commercial you can do at least a couple of ribs. Halftime is worth about five, depending on the length of your nacho and cola break. Overtime and you can finish the whole wing (just kidding).

Some places don't lend themselves to building. The stiffeners for the ailerons are already formed and pre-punched, but you still have to smooth their edges. Taking them and some sandpaper out of your carry-on bag while in seat 14B (the middle seat) on an airliner...well, you can feel 14A and 14C looking at you from the corners of their eyes. I put the stiffeners back in the bag and read my plans instead. It was a real conversation stopper. I'm not sure how it happens—it's symbiotic or something—but you can feel what 14A and 14C are thinking—"Weird!"

You can get away with the above in airline crew ready-rooms, however. The EAA sticker on your flight bag gives you license to pull out just about any airplane tool or part from of your bag. The response in the ready-room is usually, "Cool!" "Cool" is a lot better than "weird."

Okay, some of you might think I'm obsessing, but I beg to differ. I'm just doing what I like to do. I like to build airplane parts. Emphasis on the word "parts." I have no timeline for completing my airplane; I know that when I get all the parts together, it will be an airplane. Meanwhile, I enjoy making the parts and completing one motivates me to start the next one.

If I'm working in the garage at 5:30 p.m. and my bride opens the garage door, home from work, I stop—90 percent of the time. The remaining 10 percent of the time I'm up to my elbows in something and can't turn loose for another 10 or 15 minutes. Then I rush inside and tell my bride of 32 years about all the great and wonderful places we're going to fly to in the RV-8. (How is it that wives can roll their eyes so effectively?)

And there is a whole list of places where I haven't taken airplane parts with me. I haven't taken them when we go out to dinner. Our oldest son is getting married in July, and I'm not planning on taking any parts to the wedding. There, that's two places right off the top of my head! I'd give you more, but you know how magazine editors are; they're always waiting for that next article and I have to get this one in the mail.

I'll admit to one fantasy time line. After I set brakes on the airliner for the last time (due to the FAA's dumb age-60 rule—not to get political or anything), I'll walk down the jetway stairs and hop in my RV-8 parked nearby, and my bride and I will fly into our retirement/sunset. Not a bad thought, huh? That time is some five years away, however. That's still quite a few layovers. I figure the airline ought to get to see my airplane. By the time I finish it I will have built about half of it on their time.

Come to think of it, I'm pretty sure I could mount an engine in a motel room. I just haven't figured how to get it through airport security

Last but not least, I really am going to fly my bride to some neat places. (Like Oshkosh, where she'll meet other goof-balls like me.) We'll go out to dinner and, you watch, there will be some guy there working on an airplane part and I'll say, "Look at that! What a jerk!" And then I'll say, "You're so cute when you roll your eyes."

8

ENTERTAINMENT VALUE

What does one do when sitting in the left front seat of an airliner on those long flights when you're on top of the clouds, the air is smooth, the seat belt sign is off, and you've finished your cup of coffee? Not to worry, just listen to the radio. The entertainment value is immense. What follows are examples of stuff heard…intentional or unintentional, I'm not quite sure. But when it happens, it brings a smile to your face and, sometimes, some snide comments from your fellow pilots. Regardless, these communications are all a part of "the pilot's life."

An airliner was asking the tower for verification of a landing clearance, "Tower, are we cleared to land on 26 Right?" The tower replied, "You would be if we had a 26 Right." Oops.

An airliner asked Seattle approach for Seattle tower's frequency and got this reply, "Nineteen-nine, same as it's been for the last 20 years." Ouch.

Oakland center asked, "Airliner 234, do you show yourself at FL290?" The reply, "Well, I'm not showing myself, but I am level at two-nine-zero." No comment.

"Airliner 123, how's your ride?" Answer, "Well, we're in occasional intermittent chop." Pause, then, "Or maybe it's intermittent occasionally. It's…well…whatever. You get the drift." None of that is exactly like it is in the AIM (*Aeronautical Information Manual*), but, yeah, we get the drift: It's bumpy once in a while every once in a while. Or something like that.

This happens a lot in the new high-tech world of flight management systems and GPS: "Airliner XYZ, you're cleared direct MUKLK." Always, crews reply, "Roger, cleared direct (mumbling now) MIKLK." Then there is a long pause, which, in the cockpit, translates to frantically pulling unfolded charts out of flight bags and running one's finger all over the chart looking for MIKLK. When one can't find it, one sheepishly asks, "Uh, Center, how do you spell MIKLK?" Center replies, "Mike Uniform Kilo Lima Kilo." (Often one can hear snickering in the background of the transmission.) "Roger, thanks." Now the pilot types in the correct fix, hits "enter," pushes "direct," checks the course line to see if it's going kinda-sorta where he wants to go, then folds up his chart and stuffs it back in his flight case. Another close call averted. Except that everybody on the frequency heard the exchange and knows *exactly* what just took place.

Landmarks can cause embarrassment, too. Coming out of Seattle on a beautiful, clear morning: "Center, TWA (may it rest in peace) 678, is that Mt. Hood in front of us?" Center replies, "Nope, Mt. Rainier, the second highest peak in the lower forty-eight," hinting at its prominence. Okay, honest mistake, but don't expect your fellow pilots to let it slide. Much chatter followed, "Don't get out much, huh?" And, "Don't got no mountains in Kansas, Toto?" All calls are anonymous, of course. The TWA crew just had to grin and bear it. One learns early on that you can't be thin-skinned *and* be a pilot.

Turbulence increases radio chatter tenfold, as in everybody wants to know, "Where's the smooth ride?" So, center often asks, "Lear 321, how's your ride?" Lear replies, "We're gettin' beat like an ugly dog." "Ugly dog" is not in the AIM either, but I'd ask for vectors around where the Lear was 'cause I think I get his drift. And, with apologies to the animal rights activists, we often say, under duress, things we neither mean nor practice. I'd be willing to bet that the Lear pilot, once he got out of the turbulence and on the ground, went home and *hugged* his ugly dog.

Overheard on a company frequency from operations to Alaska 678, "678, you're gonna hafta move four people up to first class for weight and balance." So four lucky souls got to move up to the big leather seats where the linens and roast beef reside.

Then there's the cute stuff. "Navajo 456, San Jose tower, you're cleared for takeoff 30R." And the Navajo pilot says, "Into the air for 456." Cute isn't always cute, but sometimes a little levity can be a good thing.

Then there's the dreaded, "Airliner 123, I've got a re-route for you. You ready to copy?" Airliner replies, "Yeah, go ahead," and proceeds to copy the re-route. Then, about five minutes later, he comes back with, "Center, this re-route is way out of our way and will make us late." And, "I've been coming out here for seven years and have never had this re-route." Center came on to explain, politely, that his job is to separate airplanes, and tonight, this is what he had to do…and that's the way it is. Of course, every airliner after that said, "Center, I've been coming out here for seven years and never had 'that' altitude or 'that' frequency." Sympathy for a whining pilot is a very elusive thing. Finally, one pilot broke the ice with, "Center, on a lighter note, could Alaska 543 request FL310?"

Along the same lines—I can't remember if I've told you this story and apologize if I have, but I love it—one night, going into Portland, Oregon, every time an Apache pilot acknowledged an instruction, he would follow it with "okey-dokie." It was, "Roger, Apache 123 descending to 3,000. Okey-dokie." And, "Apache 123, roger, turning to zero-nine-zero. Okey-dokie." Well, you guessed it. Pretty soon, *every* airplane on the frequency was saying "okey-dokie" at the end of their transmissions. The controller, I imagined, had bumps on his forehead from banging his head on the table in front of his radarscope. It was kind of funny.

Back to airliners. "Airliner 789, we show you 300 feet high." Now, since time immemorial, since the beginning of mankind, *never* has a pilot admitted to being off altitude. Not since ancient Egypt. It's always, "Ah, center, we show ourselves right on." Yeah, right. Only this time the "right on" was followed a little later with, "Ah, center, we're making a s-l-i-g-h-t (emphasis on *slight*) adjustment to our altimeter." Uh huh.

I have this theory about radio usage. It doesn't apply during the busy times because then everyone's listening. But during the en route quiet times often when you check in, if you talk too fast, center doesn't answer. I think it's because they're in "rest mode." Sometimes they come back with the "I was on the land line" thing (much the same as when pilots say, "We show ourselves right on altitude"). But my theory is that when I check in on the frequency and talk really slow, "Center…Airliner…234…checking in…level…at…FL330," I've entered their psyche and stayed there. Ninety-nine percent of the time it works. They answer, thinking I'm sure, "Get this guy out of my headset!"

Okay, okay, I know, we airline pukes miss a lot of en route radio calls, too. It's because we're talking. As in carrying on a conversation. And our response, in the cockpit, is usually, "How in the heck do they expect us to carry on a conversation with all these frequency changes?" Indeed.

And, oh yeah, I'm no saint in all this, either. I once gave a post-flight briefing to the passengers…or so I thought. Actually, I gave it to ground control. Her reply was, "Thanks, that was nice but I'm not going anywhere today." Mercifully my fellow pilots on the frequency didn't say anything (go figure), but I could *feel* their smirks. Whatever, "that was nice" from ground is a whole lot better than hearing "call us on the land line when you get in." Anything's better than that. Instead of "that was nice," she could have said, "that was stupid." And she would have been right.

9

DINNERTIME AT OSHKOSH

Dinnertime at EAA AirVenture is when people relive the events of the day. It's when the repository of experiences are re-told, a fun time, especially if you're just listening, which I was.

I was at the Charcoal Pit, just off the end of Runway 9. I sat alone, a "single at table 20" was how the hostess described it to the waitress. I knew the Charcoal Pit had to be okay. On the wall hung a picture of the youth soccer team it sponsored, a group of smiling young boys and girls in blue jerseys, with the coach in a tank top that said "Hawaii" on it standing behind them. It was a regular kind of place.

All tables were full, and the rumble of conversation was everywhere. I wasn't eavesdropping, but I heard. As I relaxed, sipping an "adult beverage," I took it all in. It was aviation ambience at its finest.

Gazing about the room, I noticed the stories T-shirts and hats told. A young person in a B-17 T-shirt was honoring the airplane. An elderly person in a B-17 T-shirt—the lower portion of it a bit more taut than the one the younger person wore—might have been a former B-17 crew member. Sitting on a head of gray hair, a blue hat that said "F8F" suggested that the ol' boy probably at one time flew the F8F. Any way you look at it, you gotta love it.

At the table across from me two gentlemen were saying something to the effect that if they write it, "It'll sell 50,000 copies." They had to be talking about an airplane book. They had airplane T-shirts on, but I couldn't make out the type because they were sitting sideways to me. I may never know if they get "it" written, but more power to them.

At the table in front of me were five guys whose conversation indicated they were developing some sort of flight-planning software.

They were heavy into how to make the program even better when a customer swung by their table and said, "I can't get it to do such-and-such." They were all over that with helpful suggestions and an invitation to "stop by the booth tomorrow."

Aviation businesses want and need feedback. Most aviation businesses are as much about passion as business. I'd "plug" the flight-planning software people but the logo print on their shirts was too small to read from afar. Let that be a lesson: If you want a plug, make the writing on your T-shirt large enough to read from the next table.

Sitting behind me was a guy talking about an 800-foot airstrip he called to have put on an aeronautical chart. The 'chart people' put it on the chart all right, except that they listed it as an 8,000(!)-foot strip. Oops. He got it straightened out after what he called an "interesting journey through bureaucracy."

When the two gentlemen at the "It'll sell 50,000 copies" table stood up to amble out, they were still discussing a bevy of ideas for their publication. Shortly after the table was cleared, four young men took their places at it. They ordered beverages, and when their drinks arrived, they hoisted them, clinked their glasses in the center of the table, and, in unison, said, "To Oshkosh."

That sort of says it all, doesn't it?

As I left my table an elderly African American gentleman sat down, his hair sprinkled with gray. No T-shirt, no ball cap, just nicely dressed. He laid a book on the table. I could only make out two words on the cover. One was "wings," and the other was "war." Was he a World War II vet? Probably. Tuskegee? Dunno. I so wanted to talk to him, but I didn't want to intrude. I'm in awe of the Tuskegee Airmen. A group of young men told "no" at every turn, in large part because of their...pigmentation!??! Pure, unadulterated balderdash. Yet they persevered, overcame, flew, and fought for their nation. Driven by what? Pride? Love of the sky? Love of their country? I can't be sure, but whatever it was, I'd like to have a 50-gallon drum of it at the ready at all times.

Through all of the goings on I noticed something else: politeness. There were a couple of restaurant order mix-ups, but through it all there was only "hey, that's okay" and "no problem...I'll just eat this instead." No outbursts, no impolite displays of self-importance, just people among people, treating each other with respect. What's up with that? Is it the festiveness of the show? A characteristic of airplane people? Of EAA people? I guess I don't know. But I do know that I like it. Pleasant people evoke pleasant feelings.

I had another vignette to share with you, but it got smeared. You see, I took notes for this story on the paper place mat at the table. I was able to read all my scribblings, except for the three-word note that got covered by a large drop of Ranch dressing. Wiping the drop away only made it worse. Sorry, but whoever you were, your story got smeared. A thousand apologies. I'll try and eat more carefully next time.

No Oshkosh story would be complete without mention of the trip to and from. I rode United Airlines jump seat from Portland, Oregon, to Chicago, Illinois, and back. You know it's going to be a good trip when you step into the cockpit and see the captain's flight bag has an EAA sticker on it. That's what happened on the trip east. Jeff was in the process of re-covering his Christen Eagle, and Alan had a restored Cessna 140. (Note to Jeff's wife: Yes, he showed me pictures of you and the kids, too.)

On the return trip, Steve and I talked of Vietnam and rodeo. I'm afraid I didn't get the first officer's name because, I guess, Steve and I sort of dominated the conversation, being the same age and all. Sorry. In Vietnam, Steve was what the Army calls an "eleven bravo" (11 B). That's military talk for infantryman. I was a pilot in Vietnam. Those guys in the rice paddies had it a lot harder than I did. The crews I rode with couldn't have been nicer. Aviation is a brotherhood. We flew for different airlines, but when we parted we shook hands and wished each other well. And we meant it.

Sure, Oshkosh is about the show, the Tuckers, the Wagstaffs, the Franklins. But it's a lot more than that. It's about being there, building, restoring, and supporting the entire endeavor. It's about the people who come and watch. Everybody is a participant. Everybody is somebody. And that's exactly what makes Oshkosh, well, Oshkosh. You!

10

PERSPECTIVE

I like this flying thing that we do. So do you. It's one of the reasons why we're EAA members, immersed in it. I like aviation for a lot of reasons: the science and mechanics of it, the challenge of doing it right, and the people one meets. But there's another reason that often captivates me: the *perspective of life* that flying gives. Such a perspective grabbed me several nights ago as I descended into the Los Angeles area. When it happened, I knew I had to share it, to see if you agree with me, to get your reaction. We are, after all, pilots and bonded as such.

It was a crystal clear night, and the Los Angeles basin, huge, sparkled below like a carpet of jewels. It glistened and flickered and spoke of many things, of lives and careers gone by, of lives beginning, of hopes and fears, of good, bad, triumph, and tragedy, of sin and salvation. It was life displayed on palette earth, a diorama, a microcosm. It was all of these things. It was there for us to see and reflect upon because we fly.

It got me to thinking: I once watched a TV documentary about kids growing up in a Los Angeles ghetto. When a child did well in school, the older kids ridiculed him, so he quit trying. Broke my heart. I would love to have that child in my cockpit, to lift him above it all, to show him that there is life elsewhere, everywhere, where he can blossom and shine. I wanted to give him perspective.

In the big picture, there are some very large cities, but all have roads to and from them. If one doesn't work, try another. From above, roads are the umbilicals and arteries and veins of the landscape, connecting us and holding us together. It's all a part of the ebb and flow of life that we observe from above. Look down and problems seem smaller. Look up and problems can be overcome.

I need to backtrack a bit. From a high altitude on a clear night Los Angeles was nearly spiritual, but so, in a different way, is lifting off from a small airport in a small airplane. I like the patterns that reveal themselves—patterns of agriculture, of roads and towns, of cars and trucks going to and fro. Flying never makes me feel detached, only an observer. But it always makes me feel that I am but a small part of the whole. We're *all* a small part of the whole. That concept is so much easier to grasp when you fly.

Then there is the nature aloft part of it. Be alone in a fighter at night at 35,000 feet and watch a full moon climb over a solid undercast, casting a peach-colored blanket on the cloud tops. Moon, man, and machine sharing a private, fleeting, galactic moment. Or be at 41,000 feet over Texas and *still* be looking up at the top of a thunderstorm. Moments like that let you know who's boss.

Or observe from aloft a sunset on the ocean's horizon, the sun casting a last ray of light on a coastal town settling in from a day's work. Or be between layers of clouds in early evening, and observe the kaleidoscope of colors that is a sunset, fire and ice all at once. Or be between layers late at night, overcast above and undercast below, and *feel* total darkness. Just you and the science of flight: physics, instruments, and engine. You marvel that it all works, and you're thankful that it does. It's nice, in this day and age, to be thankful from time to time. Being inside a cloud at night can make you thankful. Throw in some lightning and you also become humble. Thankful and humble, those are good things. Flying offers them up in large servings.

In daylight the vastness of our land makes itself known. The deserts of Nevada are stunning. I cross the Cascade Range from the south and, looking north, see Mount Bachelor, Three Sisters, Mount Jefferson, Mount Hood, Mount St. Helens, and Mount Rainier, all in a snow-capped row, nature's necklace resplendent above its mountain forests. Over the vast fields of wheat and corn in Washington and Kansas I marvel at the few buildings way out there, far from towns and cities, that are home to those who farm these lands. I admire their hard work and envy them the natural quiet that is just outside their back porch screen door.

Don't get me wrong, my mind often waxes nostalgic when I fly, but one burp from the engine and I'm instantly back to the task at hand. Or when the rapid-fire chatter of Los Angeles approach control crackles in my headset telling me to turn, descend, slow down, speed up, look for traffic, turn again, and descend some more, my ambience goes away in a millisecond. There are times to reflect and times to tow-the-line. I'm just glad that there are times that I *can* reflect.

The Canadian Rockies, now there's pause for reflection. Vast and remote and beautiful and forbidding and humbling and awe-inspiring. I'm pretty sure there are places there where man has never set foot. Bold claim? I know. Fly over them someday, and you'll know exactly what I'm saying. They're so vast that there are probably some unnamed peaks. I'm pretty sure I could name a peak after you and nobody would object, and your family would think it was really cool.

Or look at Lake Tahoe from above on a bright, sunny day. It's a polished mirror reflecting the beauty that surrounds it. It shines in the sun like the Hope diamond shines in the light. It is the crown jewel of the Sierra Nevada's.

And you can view society and the economy from above. Let down, north to south, over the San Francisco bay area—the Golden Gate Bridge, Oakland, Palo Alto, Stanford University, and the Silicon Valley of San Jose—at 6:30 p.m., and every freeway in every direction, as far as you can see, is solid headlights and taillights. "Don't think oil's important? Look down there," I say to my first officer. "Exactly," he replies.

Right, wrong, or indifferent, it's who we are. It's the nest we've made for ourselves, because we could. And it's a nest we'll survive. We've re-forested, we've reclaimed farmland, and we've created livability, so too can we manage our energy. Viewed from above, we are an industrious, resilient, familial species. I see it on a daily basis from 40,000 feet. That's my perception. We'll be okay.

Speaking of perspective, we get it from the people we fly with, too. I have to tell you about Gabriel. He was my first officer on an evening, two-hour flight. When we first met I could tell he was a special person. Gabriel grew up in Ethiopia. His father had some land and some cows and chickens. When the Communists took over, Gabriel said they took his father's land and livestock. Just took them. No recourse. No nothing.

Gabriel remembers being in a class of five students and only three books. They took turns studying the book on a schedule. One of his times was 3 a.m., and Gabe got up at 3 a.m. to read. From there to first officer at an airline in America. That tell you something about the guy?

Gabriel recently read in a newspaper about a school district saying it didn't have enough money to buy new books. He said, "It's not about the money. Education is in the heart." Then he added, "I can go to any library in America and borrow a hundred books."

As we fly along, me feeling proud to know this man, looking at the many lights from the many small towns in central California, Gabriel says, "This is a great country."

Now *that's* perspective.

11

FATHER

He never wanted me to fly. He never openly discouraged me, but he never encouraged me, either. Every time I'd hang a new model airplane from my bedroom ceiling, he'd buy me a new chemistry set, biology set, or Erector set. Diversions, I guess you'd call them.

The chemistry set came shortly after I'd hung up a sleek F-86. I could pour stuff in test tubes, and it would bubble and turn colors, but it didn't wow me. The fish eggs in the biology set never hatched, and I just built more airplanes with the Erector set.

I'm talking about my dad. He passed away recently. Eighty-five. Fought the valiant battle, but there are only so many indignities a body can take in one lifetime.

I'm not exactly sure why he didn't like flying. I vaguely remember one story he told of going for a ride in "some sort of Cub" with a friend, and the friend took his hands off the controls and held them up in the air while they were flying. My dad didn't say it scared him, but it probably did. He did say he didn't like it. Sometimes, single moments can have lifetime effects.

Whatever, the die was cast in his being—and in mine. I just kept building models, flying them around the house with my hands, and hanging them from the ceiling...and dreaming. Flying is all I ever wanted to do. Rebellion isn't what made me do it; I was way too young for that. It was just me. I could sometimes sense my dad's chagrin, but, like I said, he never openly discouraged me.

Like any newly minted private pilot, right after I got my ticket I rented a Cessna 172, and the relatives came for their ride with "the new pilot." I took my mom and my grampa first. My mom sat in the back, grabbed the back of the front seat, and said, "Don't go tipee! Don't go tipee!"

My grampa, 78, sat in front—his very first airplane ride—said nothing, and just looked outside. Later, on the ground, he asked my mom, "I thought you said the boy knew how to fly. How come he was reading the book before he took off?" (I was reading the checklist.) When it was my dad's turn, he wouldn't go. "If man were meant to fly, he'd have wings," he said.

Over the years I flew in and out of the local airport many times. I'd always ask my dad if he wanted to go for a ride, but he never did. His lumbago or his arthritis or his trick knee were always bothering him. He had none of those ailments. He just didn't want to go. Fine. I took it a little personal in my early days, but later I didn't. It was just him.

He came to my graduation from U.S. Air Force pilot training. He and my mom got the full tour. I think he was impressed with all that goes in to learning to fly a jet fighter. He'd never really thought about flying in that way. He wasn't a demonstrative person, but in the same way I sensed his chagrin, I also sensed that he was proud of me. I liked that.

It didn't help that while I was in Air Force pilot training, my older brother, an Air Force captain, was killed in an airplane crash. That was beyond-words difficult. I couldn't stop what I was doing; it was my life. I kept flying. But, upon graduation, in deference to my parents, I chose to fly transports rather than fighters.

It was one of the biggest mistakes of my life.

I learned too late: You must live your own life. I disliked flying transports; fighters were who I was. Later I volunteered for any fighter going to Vietnam. But in the military, once you get going down one track, it's hard to get off. I had to resign from active duty and go into the National Guard to get back to single-pilot flying. I never told my parents why I did what I did. I did it for them, but it was my mistake—and mine only—to make.

I did get to give my dad an aerial salute once. He had just returned home from heart surgery. I was returning from a mission in my National Guard airplane. I canceled IFR for about 5 minutes, dropped down, and flew right over his rural home on the hill. My pass made enough racket that he came out on the balcony. On my second pass I could see him standing there, in his bathrobe, waving feebly. He called me that night and said, "That was pretty neat." I think that's the most he ever said to me about my flying.

Several days after the "fly over," the local newspaper published an editorial about a government airplane "flying intrusive grid patterns" over the valley. My dad got a big kick out of that. Six years later, after I retired from the National Guard, I wrote a letter to the editor, saying, "Sorry, just a local boy turned pilot paying an aerial tribute to his dad."

My dad was an enigma in a lot of ways, not just about flying. He ran away from home at an early age, lived with Indians, did rodeo, and never graduated from high school. Yet he was a Cambridge University Man of Achievement and was listed in the 1981 *Guinness Book of World Records* as the "most prolific living novelist" with 850 titles.

Yeah, you read that right: 850 novels! I don't know what the final count is, but he talked often of reaching 1,000. I'm sure he made it. Most of his books were Western fiction, drawn from his Indian and rodeo experiences. He used 70 different pen names, but most were under his own name, which is why I use Jr. with my name.

He wrote a thousand books; I've written two. But he was kind of proud that I took up writing. One of my essays, "Tractors," was included in one of those big coffee table books, called *Vintage Farm Tractors*. He liked that. I quoted him in, *If Airplanes Could Talk*: "My ol' pappy used to say, if your lifting surfaces are going around, you're in a spin. He wasn't fond of helicopters."

That was an understatement. He wasn't fond of any "flying machine," as he called them. In *Man Things,* I spoke of how he and I, on the farm, dug a jillion postholes with a crowbar and a shovel, and how we pondered a lot of world problems while we dug.

But there was one problem we never did solve: "How come, if you dig the dirt out of a hole and then put a post in the hole, you never had dirt left over after you put the dirt back in the hole around the post? We never did figure it out. Figured everything else out, but not that. It remains one of life's mysteries." He liked that passage.

My dad could be quite a kidder. Not long after my bride and I got married we were riding home from the airport with my parents, and as we came over the hill that led down into the rural valley where they lived, he turned and said to my new Texas bride, "First time a Paine's ever married out of the valley." It wasn't true, but it got her attention. She learned early on to flick it right back at him. He loved it.

I think one of his crowning achievements was teaching my sons to spit. Not just to spit, but to spit for distance and accuracy. They learned and they were proud (and dehydrated). And he was proud. It was a cresting "grandparent moment."

His mind was active to the end. He worried after September 11 that the military was going to call me back to duty. "They need pilots," he said. I told him that if the Air Force called I'd go, but, really, the government didn't need old pilots. He wasn't convinced until I told him, "The chances of them calling me are about the same as the chances of them calling you." He said, "Well, that ain't too likely, then."

My dad was a horseman, rancher, and writer. He was not a mechanic. We have a framed picture I call "The Great Tractor Passing." It's a picture of my youngest son, my dad, and me. In the background is the 1953 Ford tractor that's been in the family for as long as I can remember.

One day when he knew he was really sick my dad called and said, "Come get the tractor." I had once told him I wanted to restore it. He had put a new coil on it. The new coil didn't fit the old bracket. He didn't get a new bracket. He wedged a piece of wood between the old bracket and the new coil. It worked. It's still there. I'll probably leave it there. The tractor is in my hangar, and when I'm finished restoring it, I'll use it. And I'll think of him when I do.

Okay, thank you for indulging me. I tell the story not to make you sad or to take advantage of my venue, but to honor my dad. And I tell it because you are my friends and understand. No one gets through this life without some pain, so we share, we reflect, we remember, and we press on. Thank you for listening.

Sure, I'll miss him. He was a character, independent and opinionated, but I'll tell ya what: He lived life on his terms and only his terms. Not too many of us can say that. And I'll tell you something else: When he passed, he *flew* out of that body of pain he was in. He flew again at last. To him I say, "Good flight!"

12

PERIPHERAL KNOWLEDGE

When building or restoring an airplane you learn a lot. Stuff you never knew. You learn from reading, talking, doing, practicing, and, of course, your mistakes. You gain new skills. And that's a good thing. You also have to spend money for new tools—often requiring spousal approval—and new tools are a good thing. Actually, new tools are nirvana. Facing a difficult task with a "just right" tool in your hand to make the job easy is, well, better than yoga or ten psychiatrists.

So, here you are in your shop/garage/hangar, working away with your airplane tools, working on your airplane, when it happens: your wife (aka Princess Bride of 34 years) walks in and says, "I'd like some new hanging lamps over the kitchen island." You think to yourself, I've got to finish putting the F-804Ms with the F-804L between the F-804A and B subassemblies, not to forget the F-849, and use AN3-33A bolts with AN960-10 washers and AN365-1032 nuts. But you say, "Sure, Babe. Let me take a look at it."

You go into the kitchen and take a look, and you see recessed lighting already installed above the kitchen island. You think, hmm, it's already wired. Good. All I'll have to do is hang the lamps from the recessed lighting locations. And then your warped little airplane-pilot-brain lights up with, 'Hey, I'll make a bracket with airplane scrap aluminum and with airplane tools. Oh, this will be soooooo cool, total justification for the $3 million I've spent on tools.'

Sweet Spouse, already knowing the answer, then asks, "Can you do it?"

"*Can I do it? Can I do it?* Can the man of many tools and new skills do it? Does the bear potty in the woods?" you reply in your best James Earl Jones voice. And then you add, perhaps overstating your case, "Easy."

The stage is now set: it's put-up or shut-up time. Actually, you're relishing the moment because it's show time! Out to the shop you go and gather aluminum scrap, snips, the rivet squeezer, dimple dies, the drill, countersinks, and various and assorted rivets. You bring all this into the house with great fanfare, muttering, ostensibly to yourself but actually in the direction of Sweet Spouse, "Sure is a good thing I have these tools and stuff to do this." You lay everything out on the kitchen island; it's an impressive display of tool-mania. You don't have to speak now; the tools speak for themselves. Bride's raised eyebrows and sideways glances speak to the fact that she is somewhat impressed. You think, 'Ah, desired effect realized.'

You get to work and cut the scraps to length to make a brace. Countersink the .063-inch aluminum and dimple the .025, very important to use every tool you've brought in. Overkill is appropriate in this instance. Pop in some rivets and brandish, yes, brandish the rivet squeezer in all its shiny glory to secure the new brace with AN470AD4-5 and AN426AD3-5 rivets. Your creation is strong, an engineering masterpiece. It even works. You impress yourself, although you go to great lengths not to show it (but you do feel it). In no time at all the lamps are hanging over the kitchen island, ready to illuminate the morning hot cakes or the evening stir-fry, not to mention any and all holiday feasts.

You sit a spell with your sweet (and amazed) spouse, admiring the new lamps and leaving the tools on display a while longer. All subtlety is out the window now. The ensuing conversation is sprinkled with names like Avery, Aircraft Spruce, Aircraft Tool, Wag-Aero, Van's, and Wicks. When you notice your bride's eyes rolling toward the ceiling, being an astute observer of the obvious, you know it's time to exit stage left. There is no great applause to speak of but you feel good about your performance. A little overstated perhaps, but it sure was fun while it lasted.

And then there was the time your bride was backing the truck out of the garage and the garage jumped over and ripped the right-side mirror off the truck. Bad garage! You dutifully trundle on down to the local auto dealership and ask, "Got a right-side mirror for a '99 King Cab pickup?"

"Electric? Fully adjustable?"

"Yeah."

"Yup. Two-fifty."

"Two-fifty what? Nickels?"

"Dollars."

"Dollars? As in two hundred and fifty dollars?"

"Yup."

Here's what you don't say: "I could buy an accelerometer and an altimeter for $250." (Okay, not true, but the situation begged for overstatement.) Here's what you do say, "Thanks. Have a nice day."

On the way home your airplane-brain kicks into high gear. The light comes on: Pro-Seal! The stuff you seal airplane fuel tanks with. That stuff is so sticky you could stick the palm of your hand to your forehead if you wanted to. And the mirror didn't shatter; it only broke from its mounts when the mounts broke. So…apply Pro-Seal to the back of the mirror, put it back in the mirror holder, jump in the driver's seat to check the mirror position, get back out to readjust the mirror, get back in the driver's seat, get back out to the mirror…you get the picture.

Fortunately, you and your bride sit in the same seat position because the mirror is now not only fixed, as in repaired, but it is fixed, as in one position. Forever. But it is usable, and you "fixed" it for pennies on the dollar. "Pennies on the dollar" for repairs is a good thing. (The caveat: Don't buy a used truck from a pilot, because if you're six-foot-six, the mirror is not going to work for you. Ever. Unless you break loose with $250.)

Your bride comes home, and you proudly display the right-side mirror repair. She asks, "How'd you fix it?"

"Pro-Seal."

She's smart, not about to get drawn into another airplane conversation, and simply says, "Cool." But then, in a moment of weakness, asks, "What's Pro-Seal?"

"Remember the stuff I ruined my favorite T-shirt with, and you washed it and the black stuff wouldn't come off, and you washed it again and the black stuff wouldn't come off, and you threw the T-shirt away, and I dug it out of the trash because it didn't have any holes in it?" She furrows her brow as you finish with, "That stuff."

She's not about to continue this conversation in its present vein. She walks in the house with, "Where are you taking me to dinner tonight?" Feisty is good.

There is seemingly no end to your airplane-building skills and knowledge. You press on ready to repair the world with your airplane tools. When the fountain/water feature on the back deck springs a leak, it's Pro-Seal Man to the rescue, once again dressed in your black-stained but still good T-shirt. And when you need to repair the hole where that stupid gate ripped the headlight off the tractor, maybe you'll use some aluminum sheeting and blind rivets or a fiberglass lay-up.

Whatever, the point is made, again and again, repairs are made, fixes are tendered, situations are solved, and the world is a safer and better place because you are an airplane builder with tools. Overstated? Well...yeah. But we are happy and harmless creatures.

13

HAPPINESS IS.....

We've all slammed on a couple landings that we're not too proud of. And we've been at 12,000 feet, over the mountains, when the ice was building on the wings and it wasn't comfortable. And we've had that "surprise" annual that hit us right square in the wallet when we least expected or needed it. But, ya know, we just keep coming back for more, don't we? We just keep flyin'. And I think I know some of the reasons why. There's a lot about aviation that makes us feel good. I've compiled a list of some of those things. See if you agree with me. But, please, read slowly and savor.

Happiness is……..

A smooth landing in the touchdown zone.

Breaking out of the clouds on approach and being on centerline.

A smile at the gas pumps.

A flying job where the paychecks don't bounce.

An airplane that's difficult to load out of CG.

An airplane where everything installed works.

A "no problems" annual.

Breaking out on top in the sunshine.

A crew member that you get along with.

Fabric that tests good.

Smooth air and a tail wind.

Not forgetting to set the altimeter to 29.92 when climbing through 18,000 feet.

Not forgetting to set the local altimeter when descending through 18,000 feet.

Just a very few drops of oil under a radial engine.

A Stearman on a warm, calm day.

A hangar all your own.

A helpful controller.

An on-time arrival.

No fog in the forecast.

Going direct.

Smiling passengers.

Soloing your son or daughter.

A spouse who tolerates the airplane payment.

An engine that doesn't quit.

Hull insurance never used.

An uneventful flight.

A 1,000-foot overcast that is 1,000 feet thick and an instrument rating.

Ice that breaks off cleanly.

An engine that starts easily.

A brief ATIS.

A good radio.

Uncontrolled airspace.

A J-3 on a grass strip.

A car that starts at the end of a trip.

A good EKG.

A kinder, gentler FAA.

A chief pilot who respects you.

A reputation as a good pilot.

A forecast of 1/4 mile and fog that doesn't happen.

Not being furloughed.

A gift membership to EAA.

Having no need for a warning horn to go off.

Remembering to identify a VOR station.

Not busting an assigned altitude.

Your own airplane.

A good partnership.

Having no need for an aviation attorney.

Not missing a checklist item.

Eating at a small airport restaurant.

A steep turn where the altimeter doesn't move.

Skimming the tops in a fast airplane.

A student with a great attitude who puts forth good effort.

The smile after a first solo.

Reading flying stories that make you smile.

NAVAIDs that work.

No thunderstorms forecast.

No towering cumulus along your route.

A "you're hired" call from an aviation business.

A compliment from a fellow pilot.

Oshkosh.

Having the answer to some obscure aviation question.

An altitude held.

One moment of glory.

Avgas for less than $2 a gallon.

An airport courtesy car that runs and has brakes.

Listening to old-time aviator stories.

A full load of passengers.

A clearance that's ready when you ask for it.

A clearance understood.

A compliment from a passenger.

Nothing on your mind but flying.

Time, an old hangar, an old airplane, and a light, warm rain falling.

Snow-covered mountains through the tops of an undercast.

An autopilot when you're tired.

A new private certificate, a 172, a friend and a nice day.

No major screw-ups.

Accurate navigation.

Courteous fellow pilots.

Looking at the world from between the wings of a Stearman.

Someone who likes your style of flying.

A crossing restriction met.

A vector allowing for a graceful intercept of the localizer outside the OM.

A request honored.

A good ground crew.

An emergency avoided.

The sound of a radial engine.

Runway remaining.

An ETA met.

The first-class feeling after a good flight.

A passed physical for under $100.

Having "the big picture."

A written passed.

The airplane of your dreams and the money to buy it.

A clearance given at a speed you can copy it.

Not getting your radio transmission stepped on.

A start on the first pull of a hand prop.

A holding pattern gracefully entered.

Current charts.

Flying with your son or daughter in a Champ.

Hanging out at the hangar with your family.

Springtime from 1,000 feet AGL on a calm day in a slow airplane.

Powerful vistas.

Lots of flat, hard ground under you.

A good landing with relatives on board.

A Super Cub on freshly mown grass.

Still enjoying the day's flying at home at the end of the day.

Saying "see ya again soon" to your airplane as you push the hangar door closed.

An airplane that you built that flies true.

A perfect rivet.

The right tool.

The good people you meet at small town airports.

Prominent landmarks on a VFR cross-country.

Mastering your taildragger.

Touching a DC-3 and thinking of where it's been.

A B-17 flying over a flag-waving crowd.

Thinking of the EAA defending your aviation freedoms.

Learning.

Always learning.

Proficiency.

Seeing the dedicated look in the eyes of today's young military aviator.

Airpower in defense of freedom.

An airport restaurant breakfast.

Two hours of conversation about nothing alongside your airplane in a hangar.

Brats at the editor's house during OSH.

The symmetry of a Super Cub.

A row of Staggerwings at OSH.

A small town FBO operator who says, "Here…take my car to town for lunch."

Flyin' your bride for a ride.

Looking forward to your next flight.

14

FATHER TO SON

Dear Son,

Wow, a second lieutenant in the United States Marine Corps. That's awesome. And now in pilot training at NAS Pensacola. It goes without saying (but I'll say it anyway) that I'm proud of you. But, ya know, I'd be proud of you no matter what, mainly because you've grown to become an honest, productive citizen and loving husband. These are the things that matter in life, and you and your brother embody them. You guys make Mom and me bust our buttons.

But the fact that you're following the path I followed (except I took the Air Force route) compels me to offer some observations, gleaned from forty years and 17,000 hours of flying, about flying airplanes.

Some years ago when you said, "Dad, I want to learn how to fly," we bought a Champ. What a fun ride that was! We bonded with that little airplane—and each other. Even if you end up being a Blue Angel, if a Champ taxis by it'll always turn your head. It just will. At the time I wanted to instill some basics: respect the machine, respect weather, look before you turn, hard work and study, have high standards—have fun— and be on speed to land. Those basics still apply. And they always will.

But much of what I've learned over the years I've learned from others. As an instructor at the airline I began to notice that the pilots I considered very good had certain characteristics in common. I want to share those characteristics with you. Take what you will from them. You are destined to become your own kind of pilot, but having a *philosophy* of aviation is a good thing. What follows is essentially aviation philosophy.

First, let me say that the best pilots are not the most demonstrative ones. In other words, they are not the loudest ones at the bar. They are outgoing people but fairly introspective about their work.

They are what psychologists call "controlled extroverts." Thus, most of what I learned in the watching. Here's what I've observed. Good pilots…

Prepare. They come ready to fly. They know what is expected of them, and they prepare to meet those expectations. They know their limitations; they know their aircraft's limitations. And they do not cut corners.

Plan ahead. I could easily have said, "The good ones plan *way* ahead," because they do. Seldom are they caught by surprise. While involved in one task, they already have another one in mind should the present one not· work out. Their 'war stories' are usually of some mechanical failure because they seldom, if ever, put themselves in a position to fail.

Know and respect the weather. Good pilots study the weather before they fly. They are aware of worst-case scenarios and plan accordingly. Simply put, they do not leave weather to chance. And they avoid the really bad stuff like they avoid root canal work.

Look outside a lot. Almost constantly! They scan inside, but when in VFR weather, their attention is outside. Cockpit duties are done so that no one thing keeps their head down for an extended time. In other words, in flying, they are heads-up people.

Never seem to get very excited. The good ones do not rattle easily. They just work things out, bit by bit, until they get the situation under control. They exude a quiet confidence and maintain that in most situations. I guess it follows then that good pilots are generally smooth on the controls, no jerky, rapid movements, just constant attention and gentle pressures.

Are aware of their surroundings. Good pilots know what's going on around them. They know where the traffic is and how they fit in the big picture. They even anticipate ATC's needs and are courteous and helpful to controllers as well as to other pilots. They never think they are in the only darn airplane in the sky.

Are brief on the radio. They know what information the controller needs and provide it in one concise transmission, not three. And when given a frequency change, the good ones never rudely reply, "Bye."

Have a feel for their airplane. The good ones seem to know where their airplane is—how it's flying—at all times. Their maneuvers are never in doubt; the craft never flies them. It follows that good pilots are out flying. You don't get a feel for an airplane sitting in an office talking about it.

Are proud. I wanted to say that good pilots are not wimps, but in print that gives a poor connotation. By wimp, I mean too timid. The very timid say no to everything; it's safe, but it accomplishes little. Good pilots get the job done. They will go to the limit because they know what the limit is. They use, but do not abuse, limits. Minimums are sacred to them.

Are safe. It follows that pride never gets in the way of safety. They get the job done—if it can be done—with safety first.

Do not mind checkrides. Really! For good pilots it's an opportunity to show their stuff. After a checkride, if you mention an area of concern to them, they already know what they did (and probably some things that you didn't catch). The good ones set their standards much higher than the minimums, and they are open-minded about new techniques.

Are good communicators. They make it a point to ensure that everyone understands them. You know what they are going to do because they've told you what they are going to do. No surprises. And they make darn sure that they understand controllers and that controllers understand them.

Take care of themselves. Good pilots understand that when they are healthy they perform better. They go to some lengths to stay healthy both physically and mentally. They have the courage and intelligence to not fly when they know they are not up to flying.

Read. Yeah, they are always reading about aviation things. They read newspaper articles, magazines, and books. If it has to do with airplanes, they are interested. That interest pays them dividends. They are aware of all aspects of their industry. It is an awareness that pays. They are always up to date.

Have a twinkle in their eyes. It's hard to quantify or describe, but they do. They just do. They enjoy the heck out of what they're doing, and it shows in their eyes. They fly well, and it just tickles them pink to do so. They may not verbalize it, but, like I said, you can see it in their eyes.

Professional. This is the one word I'd pick to summarize the traits good pilots have. Flying is what they do, and they do it well, no matter what kind of aircraft they are flying. Many will read themselves into the characteristics of good pilots when, in reality, there are but a few who embody them all. But is that not one of the beauties of aviation? It is always challenging. We have yet to fly the perfect flight, but we should always be out there trying. That is what the good ones are doing.

Son, I have no doubt you are going to be a good pilot. You bring the right stuff to the table. Your Mom and I are proud of you and wish you well on the incredible journey you are beginning. It's a wonderful ride.

Our love and hugs to Gina, too. You can't do what you're doing alone. A professional in her own right, Gina has set high standards of her own for you to emulate. And that's *way* cool. She is so precious and easy to love. Not to mention that she baits her own fishin' hook!

Love, Dad

P.S. Wanna go partners on another Champ?

15

ICE

Ice is not my favorite subject, but only because I don't like it. It is a frequent subject, however, in the winter months when we deal with it a lot. So I'll give you my two-cents worth. You probably already know that what I have to say won't come out of any textbooks. It will come from many years of dealing with the stuff, from sitting in the left front seat and watching it smatter-up my windshield. It is from that perspective that I write.

For you rookies out there: Take off clean and if you're in icing conditions, get out.

For you veterans out there: Take off clean and if you're in icing conditions, get out.

I'm not exactly sure how it works-- it's some sort of magic, I think --but I do know that air has to flow smoothly over the top and bottom of an airfoil for an airplane to fly. Run your fingers over a smooth surface and note how gently they slide along. Now run your fingers over some sandpaper. They don't slide along so easily, do they? It is the same with air over an airfoil. If it doesn't flow smoothly, lift is degraded. It puts you closer to what those fancy aerodynamicists call "the stall." This point was recently brought home to a private pilot-- an *experienced* private pilot --when he tried to take off on a cool Eastern Oregon morning with "just a light coat of frost" on his wings. He wrote that he rolled down the runway, rotated at the normal speed to the normal attitude, then "felt a slight shudder and crunched back down on the runway." Thunk! Brakes. Stop. Embarrassment. Dang! The final words in his article were, "What I did was stupid." Uh...yeah. But what he did has been done before and, unfortunately, will be done again. Except not by *Sport Aviation* readers because they're brighter than the average bulb. I return to my original premise: Take off clean. Have I said that before?

Now let's take it to the extreme: At my airline, the Operations Manual had eighty-four (!) pages of rules for dealing with ice. The airline was very proud of it. And the Feds loved it: anything that long, with that many charts and graphs and gobbledygook has got to be good. FAA APPROVED they stamped it. Cool. Everything was right with the world. Except that it is now up to the poor working pilot to try and sort it all out and make practical sense of it. And then this twenty-six year cynical airline veteran-- me --(we flew for years without those eighty-four pages) mentioned to the 'cubicle pilot' who wrote it, "I condensed your eighty-four pages into three words." I'll leave it to you, the reader, to guess what those three words were: Hint (fill in the blanks): T_____(rhymes with 'cake') O_____(rhymes with 'off') C_____(rhymes with 'bean').

Okay, okay, I'm having a little fun here. There is a lot of good information in those eighty-four pages. And the people I poke fun at don't hate me; they know I spend a lot of time laughing at this world. And one of the reasons those eighty-four pages exist is because people sometimes *don't* take off clean. They're in a hurry, lazy, don't have the stuff to clean the wings/tail, are stupid (dare I say that?), or just don't have an appreciation for how important it is to have a clean airfoil. So the company and the Feds made compliance regulatory/mandatory at my airline. Now, if you don't comply, it's your license/career/future. That puts a whole new perspective on having a clean airplane.

Let's look at the eighty-four pages a little closer. There are charts, graphs and tables. Depending on the type of precipitation, the temperature, and the type of de-ice fluid used, you are given what is called a 'holdover time.' After de-icing, you must be airborne prior to the expiration of that holdover time or you have to come back and do it all over again. (There is a new fluid, called Type IV, that doubles holdover times; it's nifty, expensive and green....looks like you've been 'slimed' after you use it.) Too, after de-icing, a trained ground person, called a 'certified de-ice coordinator' must run his hands over the wings and tell you they are clean. That's called a 'tactile inspection.' Also, anytime the surface temperature is less than +6C and the temp/dew point is within 3C, you are required to have a de-ice coordinator do a tactile inspection, regardless of any other factors. This all serves to put someone other than the pilot in the decision chain. See what's happening here? Decisions have already been made for you in the airline business: fluid types, how long you can hold-over, ground personnel in the decision chain. It can be cumbersome, but it's all for the best. Bottom line: there are a hundred people sitting in the back of the airplane counting on you to T_____O_____C_____.

What about the private/corporate/bush pilot? The resources available may be different, but the same principles apply. However you have to do it, whatever it takes to make your airfoil smooth and shiny and to keep it that way, do it. 'Nuf said.

And keep this in mind (a quote from my book *If Airplanes Could Talk*): "If you are holding short for takeoff wondering if you have too much ice on your airplane, you have too much ice on your airplane."

Now let's go fly. Know this: If it's close to freezing on the ground and you're going to climb into moisture laden clouds shortly after takeoff, you're going to get some ice. Period. Knowing that helps you deal with it. Fortunately, the freezing level band is fairly narrow, usually only a couple thousand feet thick or so. Before you leap off the ground, you should have a pretty good idea where that level is. And, if you ask, the meteorologist will even tell you where he thinks it is. If he starts talking to you about the "adiabatic lapse rate" or uses similar, large, multisyllabic meteorological terms, change the subject. You don't need to know. All you need to know is approximately where the freezing level is.

Now that you have a rough idea where the freezing level is, you can formulate a plan to deal with it. Stay under it or go over it. In no case do you want to stay in it. What if ATC says, "No!" when you request a change in altitude? Scream bloody murder. This phrase usually works fairly well: "I want it on tape that you are endangering this airplane, this crew and its passengers by refusing our request." That may seem a little harsh, but I didn't make the phrase up. I heard it over the radio. And it was from a former controller turned pilot. I know that controllers have to maintain separation standards, but they can almost always do *something*. And, in all fairness, most all of them will anytime they can.

The next issue for you consideration is rate of accumulation. If the ice doesn't build up very fast, you have a little extra time to deal with it. If it's wham! one inch, you had best be doing something about it *now*. Right now! Rate of accumulation is not always easy to predict. It has been my experience that *most* of the time the rate is fairly predictable given the known conditions you are in. But not always. It is those 'not always' times that you have to watch for. That's why I say, "If you're in the stuff, get out."

Type if ice? I know you're going to beat me up on this, but I don't really pay too much attention to type of ice. I hear people all the time on the radio proudly proclaiming, "Yeah, one-half inch clear here." Or, "Three-quarter's inch rime here." And, from the ice aficionados, "Half inch mixed." Whatever. Ice is ice. Get out of it.

Okay, you say, what about ice protection systems? They range from none to boots to hot wings. I've used them all. I proposed to my bride in a Cessna Cardinal. Right after I proposed, I was not-- as you might imagine --giving my full attention to flying. (Gimme a little slack: I had three-hundred hours total time, okay?) Finally, I glanced out at the wing and there was a light coat of frost on the leading edge. "Oh, golly, gee whiz," I said to myself. In the Cardinal, I couldn't move the ice so I moved the airplane…..to a lower altitude. The frost went away. Keep in mind that this happened over forty years ago; it was easier to get a requested altitude because there were a lot fewer airplanes in the sky. So I learned a little about ice that day. (And, even with my aviation *faux pas,* that same girl is still with me.)

Boots? I don't want to be rude but they are, for the most part, marginal. And I've flown a bunch of them, from Navajo's to OV-1's to DC-3's to the last turboprop I flew many years ago, the DHC-8. Boots work, but within limits. A light coat of ice? Don't bother using the boots. That's why they tell you to let the ice build up. So you wait for just the right moment-- you think --and then inflate the boots. Oooops, too soon. The boots cracked the ice but didn't break it off. Now the new ice is accumulating over the old, uneven cracked ice, making your airfoil even more of a mess. I remember reading an Ernie Gann story where he talked about breaking ice off by backfiring the radial engines. Fine. But it doesn't work with a turboprop. I never tried it with the DC-3. With it, I'd open the side window to look out, freeze my fingers and nose and say, "Yup. Ice. We're outta here."

I'll tell you when boots work best: When it's +3C and you're out of IMC. Inflate them and the stuff will break off clean as a whistle. It's fun to watch that happen. Never mind that in another 2 degrees-- +5C or so --the stuff will come off anyway, all by itself. So, bottom line, the Feds say boots allow you to operate in icing conditions, but they are not the be-all-end-all, that's for sure. Take heart if you someday run into too much ice: I've seen booted airliners turn around and return to their departure point because the ice came on so much and so fast that a one-hundred-eighty degree turn was their only option.

I've been one of those airliners. A one-eighty is not a disgrace. It's a lifesaver.

Hot wings? They are the greatest thing since sliced bread. A little ice? Switches on and shortly thereafter your wings are clean. Ditto a lot of ice. You think differently about ice when you have hot wings. (You *still*, of course, have to takeoff clean.) They are a great concept and generally found only on very expensive airplanes.

This article is not meant to be a total treatise on ice. I just hit some of the basics. But the basics are important. And there are exceptions to almost everything I've talked about. Be aware of that. In fact, after I finished writing the first draft of this article several years ago for my airline, I flew a trip from Portland, OR to Sacramento, CA. We were at FL290, OAT was -15C, and we were skirting the western edges of some massive convective activity that was taking place along the Cascade mountain range. The First Officer looked out and said, "We have a little ice on the wing." What the heck??!!?? We were in the clear, for cryin' out loud. And we had been climbing in the clear. And it was too cold for ice; it's supposed to already be frozen at -15C, right? Whatever. We had ice. On with the hot wing switches and the ice went away. (I told you hot wings were nifty.) The meteorologists would probably talk to me about "convective activity" and "uplifting" and "super cooling." And I'd say, "Yup, it was all of the above." It was also an exception.

In closing, if there is any doubt in your mind about what the basics are when dealing with ice, go back and re-read paragraphs two and three. And always remember this (another quote from *If Airplanes Could Talk*): "The best ice prevention device in an airplane is you."

16

ROUND-MOTOR CLASSIC

Want to fly a real classic? An airplane that made—and is still making—aviation history? Okay, you're in luck. Today's the day. C-47. Civilian name: DC-3. Classic lines. Strong silhouette. Big. Honest. Straightforward. True. A friend. A workhorse. Sincere. No fluff. Is who it is. Your kind of airplane. A pilot's airplane. Taildragger. Proud. Sittin' on the ramp. Waitin' for you. Today, you're the pilot. It's springtime, clear and calm, with visibility a million miles.

If your heart doesn't beat a little faster when you walk up to this steed, then you aren't alive. But today, you are alive. It's an honor to be able to become one with this airplane. Anticipation fills the air—and your soul.

On the walk-around inspection, if you compare this round motor classic to a 747, it's small. But it isn't really small. In its own element, alone on the ramp, it's huge. By reputation alone it's humongous. Nose pointed proudly up, the cockpit is way up there. Long wings. Lots and lots of rivets. Fabric ailerons. Don't just look. Touch 'em. This is a hands-on airplane. Walk around the front of the left wing. De-ice boots. Shiny black rubber. Won't need 'em today. The engine. Big. Round. Cowled. A little grease and oil here and there. Wiggle the cowl flaps. Get grease on your fingers. A preflight as it should be: sharing grease and oil with your machine.

The landing gear. Big, round tires in huge forks. A huge place in the cowl for the gear to retract into. Lots of good stuff to look at in the wheel well. You bump your head in there and get a little oil on your forehead. Now you look like the pilot of a classic airplane.

You continue your walk-around. Another beautiful engine and prop. Another wing. And then the tail. Right down where you can see and touch it. Fabric rudder and elevator. Aluminum everything else.

You thump and wiggle and shake everything. Hands-on. Always hands-on. Everything thumps good.

You deem this airplane ready for flight. Actually, this airplane was born ready for flight. You clamber up the rickety ladder through the cargo door. No frou-frou jetway. Just a practical way to climb aboard. As it should be.

Clomping up the fuselage, it sounds like an airplane. It feels like an airplane. It *smells* like an airplane. No carpet. Just hollow sounding flooring and bulkheads and longerons and lots more rivets, set long ago by someone who cared about what they were doing.

You squeeze into the cockpit and settle in. The seat cushions are shiny from use, and the windshield is right in front of your face, at an angle. A slight breeze wafts through the open side window and brushes your face.

Born before ergonomics, the cockpit is home to the necessary stuff, scattered here and there. In the instrument panel the attitude indicator, big, black, and with no indexed increments, sits in the middle. A caged heading gyro is before the pilot. A hydraulic gauge, with one big needle, is attached to a line that comes up from the floor by your left elbow.

There's a plethora of throttle, prop, and mixture controls. The gear levers (plural) are behind you, one on a bulkhead, another on the floor. No flicking of levers here; you move over and down, unlatch, pull up, and move over and back again. Cumbersome? Yeah. But it works. What more do you want?

Sit a minute. Take it all in. Many have sat where you sit, with many thoughts. The Hump. The Berlin Airlift. Paratroopers on D-day. Freight in the middle of the night, lightning flashing in the distance. Old men remembering. Young people trying to imagine what it was really like. The North Pole. The South Pole. This airplane has been everywhere and done everything. Will there ever be another like it? I doubt it.

It's time to fly. This airplane was born to fly. That is what it does best. But first you have to start the engines.

Nope, you can't just push a button and move the thrust lever (Thrust lever? That's what they call 'em these days!) from shut-off to idle at 15% rotation. Nope, starting a radial is like building a house. You lay the foundation and go from there, one thing leading to another until it starts. There's as much technique as there is procedure involved. And if you backfire the darn thing, everyone within ten miles knows and you'll hear about it for years.

Get ready to start. Switches on. Some prime. Hands ready in the right places. Left engine first. Hit the start button. Look out and count the blades as the starter whines—six, seven, eight—mag on, mixture up...not too much. Cough. Touch the throttle. Puff of smoke. Still whining. Another cough. Two coughs. A little more mixture. More smoke. More coughs, *chunk, ca-chunk, ca-chunka-chunkachunka*. Mixture up, gentle throttle, smoke gives way, engine clanks, groans, and then comes to life in a deep-throated idle. Vibration. More wind in the face through the window. Success.

One more engine to go. Same procedure/technique again. More vibration. More deep rumbling music. No backfires. You're safe from ridicule one more time.

Unlock the tail wheel. Nudge the throttles forward. You begin moving. You feel every bump and wiggle. Tap the brakes. You sit high, using both feet and both throttles in coordination. Just you—arms, legs, hands, and machine all working together. Feeling your way down the taxiway. It's an honor to be steering this airplane.

Swing the tail around for the run-up. Stand on the brakes. Hold the yoke in your lap. Throttles forward. A great roar. The sinew of the monster radials reveals itself. Honest power. Eager to serve. Check the mags. Rpm drops. Rpm increases. Exercise the props. Airplane groans, then roars back to its original roar. Airplane's ready. You're ready. Everybody's ready. It's time.

Taxi onto the runway. Lock the tail wheel. Throttles up. Way up. A great roar. The wonderful noise! So beautifully loud. The roll. Yoke forward. Tail up. Tap the rudders. Goes pretty much straight. So honest, this airplane. Yoke back. Slightly back. Back a little more. Feel the weight come off the wheels. Airborne! Slightly airborne. Then a lot airborne. The ground gives way to scenery. This is why we fly. The gear: over and down, unlatch, pull up, over, and back again. The gear works its way up and you're clean, airborne. *Flying*.

The roar and the vibration! You hear it, but more than that, you feel it. The airplane flies straight and true, just waiting for you to nudge it, to tell it where you want it to go. A little heavy on the ailerons, but who cares? This airplane is about purpose.

You nudge the ol' C-47 here, and you nudge it there. Scenery. Noise. Wind. All classic...because of the machine. There are no words now. None are worthy. You are alive, made so by maybe the most wonderful airplane ever made.

I'll leave you alone now. Fly as long as you like. Do what you want. Think what you want. Just enjoy every millisecond—you're a pilot, and you're flying a classic. We'll come back and land when you're ready....

Okay, okay, I knew you wouldn't tire of it, but the fuel gauges are bouncing around between a half and a quarter. We'll do it again someday, I promise. But for now, let's head for the pattern. There is yet more airplane personality to discover.

You're at pattern altitude, on the 45-degree entry. Slow a little, props up, mixtures up. Downwind now. Gear over and down, push down, latch, over, and back again. The nose wiggles slightly as the gear stretches earthward. Engines are loafing now, just churning along easily. Golly, they're wonderful creations! Some flaps. Some more flaps. Final. All the flaps. On speed. A little more power now. View is good out the front. Engines sound about right for this speed.

The journey's end is now near. Pavement. Back pressure. Not too much. Hold it. Tail low. Throttles back. *Ca-chunka-chunka* idle. Hold it off. Hold it off. Touchdown. Pretty gentle, a very slight skip, wheels spin up, touch again, and stick. You don't move the yoke. Then, as the tail settles, you bring the yoke right back into your lap and keep it there as the tail wheel touches, bounces ever so slightly, and stays on the ground. Tap the rudders slightly to keep it going straight.

Let it slow more and then bring it to a stop. A gentle tap on the brakes and turn off the runway. You open your window again, the better to hear the round-motor symphony and feel the breeze. Taxi to the ramp. Feelin' good. Feelin' real good. Slowly roll to a stop. Hear, once more, the engines at idle. Pull the mixtures to shut-off. The engines wind down. And stop. Silence. An ever so gentle breeze again touches your face. Engines crackle. Just sit. Sit as long as you want. Take it all in and reflect. And thanks for the ride.

I've heard it said that when they take the last 747 to the boneyard, there will be a DC-3 there to pick up the crew. I believe it.

Okay, you just flew a classic, and you flew it well. Savor the flight. Next chapter we're going to switch gears. We're going to go supersonic in a fighter. Maybe even dogfight. Hint: Do some sit-ups and stuff because we're going to pull some g's.

17

FIGHTER FLYIN'

It's time. Today's the day. You're going to strap on an airplane that has few limits. A jet fighter. The frosting on the aviation cake. Sure, there is much to enjoy in aviation. Every airplane has its own personality and ambience, a J-3 off a grass strip for example. But you're a pilot; you want to experience it all.

So today is for speed and power. Today is for straight up, twisting and turning exhilaration in the cobalt blue. You're ready to experience and master a thoroughbred. Your heart beats faster. Your eyes narrow. This airplane will not tolerate incompetence or fear. You *must* be its master. You *will* be its master. You're trained, confident, and capable. Mostly, you're eager.

You don't just hop in a fighter. You suit up. You're going into an environment where no human can live without the proper preparation and equipment. Same goes for the airplane. At 40,000 feet a scant inch of canopy is between you and 55° F below zero.

First is the flight suit: fireproof, good fit, no shirttails, and lots of pockets for your stuff. You don't want anything floating around the cockpit during negative g flight. The G-suit is next. Wrap it around you and zip it up. Snug. It'll get even snugger when you pull g's and the bladders inflate around your waist, thighs, and calves, keeping the blood that maintains consciousness from leaving your brain.

Next is the parachute/ejection seat harness. It's snug, too. You don't want any slack in it when the chute opens at umpteen miles per hour. You don't plan on ejecting, but that rocket is right under your butt if you need it. Grab your helmet, and check and clean your oxygen mask in case you have any slobber left over from your last flight. Stuff your gloves into your helmet, grab your kneeboard, and head out to your aviation tiger.

You walk—stride, actually—across the ramp to your fighter. It's sleek. Purposeful. Powerful. Its crew chief meets you with the aircraft logbook. Everything's up to snuff. It's just you and the airplane now. After all, it has just one seat. *Your* seat. On the ladder you put your helmet in the cockpit, arrange the seat straps where you want them when you sit down, check a few switch positions, and step down.

You walk around the fighter. With military aircraft it's as much ceremonial as it is purposeful. The crew chief takes pride in his fighter. He wouldn't let you touch it if it wasn't ready. But another set of eyes never hurts, so you look. And you shed the world and ready yourself for the sky. Up close, every surface is smooth, every part strong. Wings look more like wedges than airfoils. The missiles remind you that this airplane is purposeful. All's well on the preflight. You knew it would be. There's a lot of pride going on here. Crew chief pride. National pride.

You climb up the ladder, step over the canopy rail, onto the seat, and settle into the cockpit. It fits. Everything's within quick reach because, sometimes, in a pinch, you need things to be within quick reach. The stick and throttle are right there, extensions of your hands and mind. You connect to the airplane: calf straps, ejection seat harness, oxygen mask, G-suit pneumatics, and kneeboard. Get your charts ready. There's no room to unfold them in the air.

Check switch positions and verify them with the checklist. Pull on your gloves. Pull on your helmet and snap your oxygen mask into place. Push the G-suit test button and feel the bladders inflate. It all feels good and right. You've done it many times before. Pull your visor down. You're now one with the machine. Matched. Mated. Ready. Life is good.

Looking at the crew chief standing in front of the airplane, you raise your finger and make a circular motion. After the crew chief repeats the signal, you punch the start button. At 15 percent rpm you advance the throttle to idle. There's no great noise, just a slight vibration as the machine comes alive.

As the engine settles into idle a slight hum courses through the airplane, giving a hint of the power available. You signal the crew chief to pull the chocks, and shortly he or she gives you a thumbs-up. You give the same back. It makes you feel good to be able to work with such fine, dedicated young people.

Not much to do during taxi. The nosewheel steering is effective and simple. You set the flaps and mentally prep yourself—you *fly* this thing. Canopy down and locked. You're ready!

On the runway centerline, you're cleared for takeoff. Holding the brakes, you look down the runway and advance the throttle to mil-power, check the engine gauges—they're good. You feel that this airplane—this *tiger*—wants to be released!

Feet off the brakes; move the throttle sideways and then over the hump. The nozzle opens, and the afterburner lights. A little more noise inside; a *lot* more noise outside. Acceleration. ACCELERATION pushes you back in the seat. Hard. Disengage the nose steering. Rudder's effective now. 80 knots. 100 knots. In your peripheral vision the scenery whizzes by.

With no angle of incidence you're a high-speed tricycle—120 knots—unless you rotate. 140 knots. Slight back-pressure on the stick. Nose wheel begins to get light. 155 knots. Rotate. Ground gives way. Your left hand switches the gear up. *Thump-thump-thump.* Three little lights go out.

More acceleration. Flaps up. Nose up. Up some more. *Way* up. 60 degrees of pitch. You're still accelerating. Still 60 degrees of pitch. You're not flying—you're *unleashed!* The altimeter's winding up faster than you can read it. You lay your head back to look to one side. The earth is rapidly falling away. It all feels so good. Through 15,000 feet now and still going dang near straight up.

You philosophize for a moment: Besides this and family and friends, what the heck else do you need? You answer your own question: Nothing. 20,000 feet. 25,000 feet. Going through 30,000 feet you gently roll upside down, lay your head back and let the nose fall through the horizon, and then roll right side up. You come out of afterburner. From brake release to now, you've been airborne 90 seconds.

But you and your steed are just getting warmed up. You move the stick left and hold it there. Using aileron you roll once. Twice. Three times. Your eyeballs are flicking left. You roll right once. Your eyeballs straighten out.

Point the nose down a little. Speed builds quickly. Pull. Look up. Nothing but blue sky over the nose. Look left. When you go vertical, roll 180 degrees, pull on the stick some more, lay your head back, and watch for the horizon. When it comes to the top of your windscreen, roll right side up and exit that half of the loop the same way you entered it. That's a Chinese Immelmann.

Lower the nose again, and throttle to mil-power. Speed builds.

Builds some more. You feel a slight hesitation. The pitot-static instruments waggle as you feel a slight acceleration as the shock wave passes. You hear nothing. The people on the ground hear a great KA-BOOM as you go supersonic. Speed is good. You slow and scan the sky. The missiles remind you to scan the sky.

There he is! The enemy! Coming head on. Closure with a capital C. Every nerve ending is engaged. Is he going to run or is he going to engage? If he engages, which way is he going to go? You have to know that to have a plan. You have about 10 milliseconds to make your plan. And be ready to make another plan 10 milliseconds later. It's about instinct now.

He passes on your left and then breaks right and down. You don't think he saw you until the last minute. That's good. Initial advantage yours. The sun's at your back. Another good thing. You roll left and keep him in sight through the top of your canopy. Pull the nose through the horizon and roll right side up, nose down and behind him.

He doesn't know exactly where you are, but he knows you're behind him. And he knows that's bad. He twists and turns. You twist and turn. The heavy g feeling comes and goes, but you barely notice it. Only the enemy matters. He pulls up, but not too much. He knows energy is king now. If he pulls up too much and gets slow, you can roll up and scissor him.

He heads for the deck. He may be faster than you there. No room for error here. You lose sight of him for an instant. Not good. Where is he? Still in front of you, you're pretty sure of that. You *hope*. You pull up and roll over to take another look.

Dang! He came out of that canyon, got behind the ridge, and is going away from you fast, on a beeline to home base. Aerial combat—jousting—isn't just about killing; it's about winning. And today you won. The sky is yours. You pull up and roll in the deep blue sky. Total elapsed time—180 seconds.

That guy will fight another day, a reminder to stay sharp. And vigilant. Always sharp. Always vigilant. That's what being good is all about. Today you were good. You head back to base. You lean forward, stretch your tight muscles, and ventilate your sweat-drenched back. You've been busy.

You enter the traffic pattern, an initial entry for an overhead break. At midfield you crisply bank left and pull. You feel a slight burble, vortexes spill from your wingtips, and your oxygen mask sags on your face.

Roll level. Gear down opposite the touchdown point. "Fall off the perch" and lower the flaps for the 180-degree turn to final. Fly 155 knots, plus 1 knot for every hundred pounds of fuel over a thousand pounds. 160 knots on final today. At that speed you don't flare, you don't float—you *arrive* at the runway. Just a puff of tire smoke punctuates the end of a successful mission. Hold the nose off as high as you can for as long as you can for aerodynamic braking.

When clear of the runway you raise the canopy, unlatch your mask, and feel the cool breeze. Taxi slowly while your body absorbs the remaining adrenaline. Reflect on your flight. Always reflect. You're only as good as your last flight. Today you did well.

Pull into your parking spot and shut down. The engine winds down to silence. Your muscles relax. The crew chief gives the "chocks in" signal and then a thumbs-up with questioning eyebrows. You raise a thumb, saying the airplane did well. The crew chief nods and gives a big smile.

Helmet off, disconnect, unbuckle, and climb out of your ship. Pat it. Thank it. You log .7 --42 minutes. Fighters aren't about building time. They're about flyin' and fightin', and you're okay with that. You can swagger just a little bit (confidence is okay, arrogance is not) to the equipment room. You hang your stuff in your locker, debrief, and head for home.

At home you pull a cold beverage from the fridge. Ahhhh! You head to the backyard deck, where your bride sits in the evening sun with her beverage of choice. The chicken is sizzling on the barbecue. You look at her and ask, "How was your day, babe?" She says, "Good. How was yours?" You say, "Good." And then you look at each other and nod with knowing smiles.

I'm tellin' you folks, a good airplane and a special bride, it just don't get any better'n that!

18

LOGBOOK NOTES

Whenever I do something stupid in an airplane or just want to remember a certain aerial event, I make a small, cryptic note in my logbook. It's usually just a word or two above the "from" and "to" line.

Occasionally I glance back through my logbook and read my scribbling, just to see if I've learned anything. It turns out some events are vivid still, others I barely remember, and still others I've forgotten (couldn't be age, could it?). But the comments entertain me. After all, they're a collective snapshot of my aviation life.

In my early logbooks I seem to have been dutiful, logging my time and writing short notes like "power on stalls" and "turns about a point." I was probably conserving ink inasmuch as it was 1965, I was in college, I could barely afford a pen, and Air Force ROTC was paying for my flying lessons.

One early 1966 entry stands out in my memory still. After the line "T-37, 1.3, local, day" I wrote "EEEEEEEE!" It was my first solo in the "Tweet." I went to the practice area and did four loops in a row. I was 22 years old and in flying heaven. Flying was all I ever wanted to do, and here I was in a jet—with stick, helmet, flying suit, and an ejection seat—and doing it! I wrote at the bottom of the logbook's page, "Life's complete."

Then a couple of stupid things: In pilot training students bragged amongst themselves about taking the T-38 to 50,000 feet. It was a marker, a milestone, or so we thought. So, solo, I took my T-38 up there. (This was before Mode C.) It was awesome, the sun was glinting off the wings, and I was feeling pretty darn cool. Then I peeled off in a 120-degree bank toward my imagined enemy below.

There isn't much air at 50,000 feet, and the abrupt maneuver disturbed what little airflow there was to the engines, and they both flamed out. "Cool" suddenly became "stupid." *Very* stupid. My first thought was, "Lauran, you worked so very hard to get here, and now you blow it by becoming dumber than a fence post. You stupid, ignorant jerk."

To make a short story shorter, I got the engines relit at 35,000 feet, came home, and landed. I parked, went inside, and said nothin' to nobody. Until now. (This happened 34 years ago, so I hope the statute of limitations has expired.)

What's funny is I remember the day I did this—and there is no entry in my logbook. I guess I wanted to make sure no one would read my logbook and notice that I had recorded my ignorance for all to see.

Jump to 1987. There's an entry over BOI (Boise, Idaho) that says "re-entry." I don't remember it now, but I must have been a little late on the letdown on that one. Okay, a *lot* late. Another Idaho entry says "30k x-wind." Again, I don't remember it specifically, but it must have been memorable on that day. Thirty knots across the runway would qualify as a memorable event.

On 2/19 there's a "#2 gen" entry. There's another on 2/20, and yet another on 2/23. Two different tail numbers. Must have had a run of bad generators in February.

"Vector" appears above SEA (Seattle, Washington). I *do* remember that. The controller gave us a vector out of traffic and then got very busy on the frequency. We were in the clouds, level at 6,000 feet, and, knowing the local terrain, headed for Mt. Rainier at 14,400 feet. Couldn't get a word in. Finally did. Controller was irritated. Then alarmed, "Turn left immediately and climb." Crisis averted. "Vector" in my logbook reminds me of that day.

"Rust" is a comment that coincides with dates. It's a frequent comment after two-week vacations. Two weeks may not seem like much, but when you fly nearly every day your hands just flow around the cockpit. That ability goes away in as little as two weeks. Fortunately, it comes back after a couple of legs.

"Mtn wave." Cryptic but memorable. That stuff is weird. It takes control of your airplane, and pilots don't like that. And you can't see it. You have to ride it—if you have room—or turn or something. I was flying a National Guard airplane that day, with an ejection seat. Comforting thought. But if I'd been in a light airplane, I'd have had diarrhea for a week.

"Grnd fog" is in the logbooks quite a few times. It's the kind you don't get into until you're at or below the published instrument approach minimums. Freaky stuff. You're the judge if the runway's visible enough to land or not. You have about 10 milliseconds to make the decision.

"Near miss." Yup, remember it well. We were doing a VOR approach through broken clouds, and the dirty belly of a VFR Cessna was *suddenly* and *clearly* visible in the top of our windshield. My co-pilot that day, Steve Allison, said, "Life is short." He passed away five years later. Cancer. But we didn't die that day. Steve was right—life *is* short.

"Beaut nite." It was one of those clear, smooth, bright moon, towns clearly visible everywhere kind of nights. You know the kind. Wonder and beauty all at the same time.

"Balloon." You know what that means: tad hot, flared late, pulled hard, ballooned up, high, out of airspeed and ideas all at the same time. But it must have turned out okay because I'm here talking to you about it.

"T-storm." That's in my logbooks a lot; I guess because they always get my attention. They're big, gray, ugly, bumpy, and spit stuff, like hail and lightning. And they'll rip your face off if you're not careful. In one place, "T-storm" is listed three days in a row. I don't like 'em! Even writing this, I'm visualizing them and finding ways to stay the heck away from them.

"Sick." Now, *that* you shouldn't do. Don't fly sick! I guess I did, and it was memorable enough to write the comment in my logbook as a reminder not to do it again. If you feel bad on the ground, you'll feel worse in the air.

"DJ glove." That's the day I found my youngest son's perfect baseball glove. It was just the one we'd been looking for, and I was excited to get it and bring it home to him.

"Bro." Took my son on an overnight trip with me. It was fun. It's good they know what the ol' man does when he leaves the house for work.

"Nse gr clpse." I remember it. National Guard airplane. On taxi, the nose gear just folded up. Brain goes, "Tilt!" View out the front is all wrong. Parked it. Went and got another airplane.

"Oil press." That's in there twice. Once on an airliner and

once on a Guard airplane. Had to shut down the engine each time. Luckily, both airplanes had two engines. Good thing. My innards aren't that strong.

"Drafted." That's when the company is out of reserve pilots and they call and tell you that you *will* fly that day. It's extra pay, but my days off are more important to me than money. I don't think I've answered the phone on a day off since.

"Pax in lav." I remember. It was a nasty, bumpy night. Passenger got scared and ran to the lavatory. He wouldn't come out. Landed with him in there. Paramedics gave him oxygen. He was okay. Felt sorry for him. Don't know if he ever flew again. Hope he did, on a "beaut nite."

"Smoke." Remember that, too. It was at the gate. A panel started smoking. Evacuated the airplane. Evacuated *us*. All felt sick. Canceled rest of trip. Made mental note of how fast smoke can incapacitate.

"Coyote." Yup, there he was, on the runway. Right in front of us. Missed him. Don't know how. But he got an honorable mention in my logbook.

"Batt hot." No, it wasn't just "the light." The battery *was* hot. The mechanic let me touch it. Lesson: Don't ignore warning lights. We didn't, but it's always worth repeating.

"Window crack." I remember. Looked up and saw a huge crack in the window. Asked, "Was that there before?" Answer, "Don't think so." Then, suddenly, it cracked bigger and then "bicycle-spoked." Good thing windshields are laminated.

"Red alert." Remember that one, too. Calgary, in Canada. Holding short for takeoff. Was told we wouldn't be cleared for takeoff because there was a "Red Alert." "Red Alert" is not in the *Aeronautical Information Manual*. Fifteen minutes later, got cleared for takeoff. Still don't know what a "Red Alert" is.

"Prpsl." Jump to May 31, 1968. Cessna Cardinal, N29402. 9,000 feet over the ABI (Abilene, Texas) VOR. I proposed marriage to Kay Lyn Statser. She said, "Only if it's forever." So far, so good. Thirty-three years now and still goin' strong.

I could go on. Thirty-five years is a lot of logbooks and a lot of notes, but you get the idea. Now go pull out your logbooks and look at the notes. It's kind of fun. It's who we are. It's what we've learned. After all, what is life but memories and experiences?

19

MOTHER

This is hard. As in difficult. And it's too soon. Way too soon. First my dad. Now my mom. Gone within one year of each other.

I struggle wondering if I should share this with you. I don't worry about your kindness; that's a known. You demonstrate it repeatedly in these pages. I worry that I'm bringing melancholy into your busy and positive lives, melancholy that maybe you just don't need today. If that's the case, I apologize. But my mom is my mom, and she's part of the reason I became a pilot. And the EAA is more than just an organization; it is family.

My mom was born in Montague, Michigan, in the house where she grew up, the second of three girls and one boy. I've seen pictures of the house. Hardscrabble. Clapboard. No paint. No grass. Corn growing in the background. Farmers, they were. Kids in overalls and Buster Brown haircuts, every one of them barefoot with a hoe in their hand.

I heard the stories that they got a penny a row for hoeing weeds. Hard, hot work. But my mom spoke fondly of those days and never complained of the work. Never. I think she loved it. And it shaped her life: She always lived rural, worked hard, and possessed an incredible maternal instinct. Later that manifested itself in loving family, friends, animals, and large gardens.

Later the family moved to Southern California where her dad milked cows (by hand) and her mom tended to the family. There she met my dad, they married, and I came along five years later.

My first memories are of life on a ranch: hay, cows, horses, chickens, dogs, tractors, and gardens. And lots of work, not to be dreaded but to be shared. We all did our part to make it work. If all I did in a day was chop weeds, then I'd done my part for that day. My mom could do anything: ride, milk the cow, cook, sew, wash, garden (*huge* garden), make cottage cheese and butter, can beans, make pickles, play baseball, make jam, shoe a horse, brand a cow, cut hair, drive a tractor, hug, and go to every Little League baseball game I ever played. No wonder I grew up happy. Hard work and love, those are the best things in life.

Every weekday afternoon at about three, a large two-engine airplane would wing its way across the big blue sky over the meadow where the cows grazed. It was something special to watch! Later I identified it as a DC-3, thanks to the airplane cards that came wrapped with a piece of bubble gum from T. Jones Store, in the nearest town (population 350) 6.5 miles away.

My mom once bought me a plastic model airplane. It was a Mr. Mulligan. With more glue on me than the model, I finally got it put together and flew it all through the house. We went on a lot of trips, Mr. Mulligan and I. Dreaming all the while.

Then she got me a Guillow's balsa model of an F-86, and I painted it silver. Staring at its slick shape for hours, I wondered if anything could be neater than an F-86! In one pitched bedroom dogfight I didn't bank hard enough and clipped the right wing on the doorway, splintering its wingtip. Broken-hearted, I ran to my mom. Sitting on my bedroom floor she assessed the damage. Finding the model's box, from some scrap balsa she cut a splice for the spar and some new ribs and stringers. Then she told me to replace the broken stuff, re-cover, and repaint. She didn't do it for me, just gave me the tools and encouragement. That's all I needed. The F-86 and I were back in the air in no time, and the skies, once again, were safe.

One Christmas I got a control-line model airplane with a real engine! Held together with rubber bands, you could crash it without breaking it. Good thing. I crashed it at least 7,839 times. A family friend then gave me a larger engine. I didn't have a model big enough to put it on, but I loved running engines. So I mounted it to my mom's garden fence. I don't remember asking about cutting into her fence, but I don't remember getting into trouble for it either. I ran that engine for hours, and I was beginning to think I wanted to be a pilot. Actually, I was beginning to think I *knew* I wanted to be a pilot.

The last to "leave the nest," I sensed it was a sad day for my mom when I left for college. She adjusted by teaching horsemanship to 4-H kids. And she raised fawns. Yeah, baby deer. The game warden would bring her orphans, and she'd raise them. At night she got up every four hours to feed them. We always had a couple deer around the house.

They were free to go, but they always stayed nearby. One used to come in the house, lie on the couch, and lick the cat.

And her horses, always her horses. One friend told me, "I'd always call her for trail rides because she never said no." Animals know people. My mom could stand by the barn, yell in a high-pitched voice, "Hello, Baby. Hello, Baby," and her horse would stop what it was doing in the field, look up, and then begin the long walk right up to her. Every time. It was a beautiful thing to watch.

My senior year of college I got my private pilot's ticket. When I came home for the summer, my mom was one of my first passengers. She sat in the Cessna 172's back seat, my grandpa sat in the front, and as I circled her friend's ranch, she said, "Don't go tipee! Don't go tipee!" She liked to look out, but she didn't like to go "tipee." It was always gentle banking after that.

She came to my graduation from U.S. Air Force pilot training, and we put her in a T-38 simulator. She figured if she could drive a tractor, why not a supersonic jet? She never said no. I once flew high over our ranch in a KC-135. She took a picture. It's of a white contrail in a deep blue sky framed between the tops of some tall pine trees. It's one of my favorite pictures. She came to my Little League games; she came to my flights. Like any mother she worried when I went to Vietnam. But we got through it.

When I married, she took my bride in like a daughter. My bride once said, "You know, in 35 years, we never had a cross word." That's sweetness.

When my bride and I bought our Stearman, we circled her house. She was in the garden, but she ran in the house, got a towel, and began waving the towel. The towel became her trademark whenever we flew over. When my oldest son and I flew over in the Champ during his lessons, out came the towel.

During her later years she made hook-latch rugs. She made me one with a biplane on it and gave it to me for Christmas. But that's not all she did in her later years: At age 70 she trained a new horse, as in broke it to ride. And it came to her when she called, "Hello, Baby!" She continued to ride horses until age 80, putting an upside-down bucket by the horse so she could step up on it to get her foot in the stirrups.

She's gone now. But not the love she gave me. That's forever, living in those she touched—and she touched many. That is the measure of a life well lived.

I can still feel her hugs, see her towel, hear her call, "Hello, Baby!" And I never go "tipee" with passengers on board. She's a large part of who I am. I figure that's a pretty good thing. If I've accomplished anything it's in large part because of her love and encouragement. *Thanks, Mom. I love you.*

Thank you, my friends, once again, for listening. My mother loved to smile. So I'll say to her now what she said to me a thousand times as she tucked me into bed as a small boy, "Sleep tight. Sweet dreams."

20

OLD HANGAR, OLD AIRPLANE

I'm sitting on an old wooden bench in an old wooden hangar. Before me is an old airplane, a B-17. It's quiet in the hangar, except for the sounds of an occasional pigeon in the rafters, some fall leaves rustling just outside the door—and the conversations playing in my mind.

Sitting here looking at the airplane, I hear many voices: The quiet, studied voices of the engineers who conceived it, the off-handed voices of those who assembled it, the concerned voices of those who maintained it, the excited voices of a crew under attack, and the reverent voices of those who walk around it now, in awe and with respect.

Yes, this airplane is talking to me, as are those who were—and are—a part of its history, for this Flying Fortress has much to tell, much to teach us.

Conceived from the need to deter aggression, particularly the Nazis goose-stepping across Europe, men gathered their thoughts, their ideas, their paper and pencils, their drafting boards, and their knowledge and came up with a fuselage, large wings, four engines, a bomb bay, and many turrets. This was a beast of burden, of great purpose, and strong enough to bring our boys home.

So many of the engineers who designed it are gone now, but I so want to tell them what a good job they did, to let them know how proud I am just to be sitting with their airplane now. This airplane made a difference, a huge difference. Thank you, engineers.

And then people converted the engineers' drawings into three dimensions. Huge plants. Many raw materials. Much planning. All done with great purpose in mind: deter aggression and preserve freedom.

Long assembly lines. Many parts. Each part, each person in the assembly chain important. Rosie the Riveter, a housewife helping the war effort by riveting skins to ribs and spars, making parts for the whole.

Nontraditional they were, but essential. And all of them proud. Often you can find the name of an assembly line worker inside some B-17 part. The name says, "I was here. I'm proud to help. I wish you well."

The assembly line voices I hear now, looking at this airplane, are talking of how the war is going, where husband, brother, son, or uncle are now. I hear them talk of faraway places, of Normandy, France, Italy, and Germany. I hear their concerns and their fears. And I hear their hopes for when their soldiers come home. And I hear the rat-tat-tat buzz of the rivet gun. This airplane is thankful for those who put it together.

I visualize this B-17 rolling out of the factory and into the sunshine. Beautiful aluminum. Powerful engines. New. Ready. Proud. Ready to do what it's designed to do. And I see mechanics in coveralls descending upon it with wrenches and rags, giving it the once over. The twice over.

These men care that this B-17 will function as perfectly as they can make it operate. They care deeply for their brother soldiers who will fly it. And they will go to almost any length, *amazing* lengths, to make this machine work well. I hear them talking, sometimes cursing at a recalcitrant cowling, a leaking cylinder, or a dropped wrench. Vociferous, these mechanics, but so very dedicated.

Again, many of the mechanics who worked on this airplane are now gone, but their memory lives in this airplane. I know they remember it, and I know it remembers them. I can close my eyes and see them everywhere, patching holes during the dark and cold nights of Europe, "Gotta get this thing back in the air in the morning. We're gonna get that munitions factory if it's the last thing we do!" I hear you, my friends!

I open my eyes and look up at the cockpit and the gun turrets. I can hear them, the crew members. And by hearing them, I can see their actions. They're scared, but brave. They want to be home with family, but they've got a job to do, and they're going to do it. Their country is depending on them.

Flying at 24,000 feet, they're bundled up in sheepskin and wool. But they're still cold. They're 15 minutes to target. They're alert to the sky, to the job at hand. Their adrenaline is high. There is fear. There are clenched teeth. There is camaraderie. There's, "Focke-Wulf, 11 o'clock low, coming up! Ready turrets!"

Turrets swivel, "I see 'em! Dammit, there are three of 'em. No, six!"

Formation lead to the formation, "Tighten up. We're in for a rough ride. Ten minutes to target."

Turrets follow the bogies. The gun clatter is loud, intense. There are flashes from the guns of the Focke-Wulfs. Heads are swiveling everywhere. German fighters everywhere. Confusion. Each man intent on his job, for that's the only way they'll survive. Some smoke from one of the fighters. Gunner doesn't think he hit it; he just thinks the German blew his engine. Gunner doesn't care; he just wants the German fighters to go away. Gunner sees another Focke-Wulf and fires. Pilot screams, "You see 'em?"

Gunner answers, "Yeah!" Gunner hits the fighter or thinks he does. Then he knows he did. The Focke-Wulf's left wing begins to shred pieces, rolls, trails more debris, and then bursts into flame, twisting in an ungainly way toward earth.

Fighter four pops up through the formation of B-17s, rolls into a 120-degree left bank, and comes back down, approaching the B-17 from the right wing—and fires. Shells hit the fuselage. The bomber shudders. Some piece of something hits the top turret gunner, penetrates his thick leather jacket sleeve. He doesn't feel it. He's cold and full of adrenaline. But he sees blood on his jacket. He doesn't tell anybody about it. It was a hit and run. The surviving Focke-Wulfs head for home. Pilot asks, "Everyone okay? Airplane okay?"

Airplane's still running good. Everybody says, "Okay. Let's go." They continue, drop their bombs, and then head for home. The trip home is mostly silent. There are many private thoughts. There is much excitement to absorb.

The silent airplane before me is telling me all this. I can hear it. And it's all true. The crew is gone now, but not their memories. Not their service. Not their honor. It's all preserved, right here before me by one old, but very proud, B-17. I am thankful.

The hangar door opens, and some people, young and old, walk in. At some point each one of them stops, takes a long look, points, and speaks. They honor this plane. They honor all who created, built, maintained, and flew it. They are thankful it is here to tell its story.

Some say it honors war. Hogwash. It honors what it takes to keep a free people free. Freedom isn't a given; it is earned. And always, always must be protected.

In the last hour that I have been sitting alone with this B-17 it has spoken to me, as have the people associated with it, and it has taught me much. It has taught me of bravery, service, and pride and love of country. And I thank it and its people for all of that.

And I'm thankful that it's restored and flying. I even worry less about the future because of it, for no one, no youth, can visit it and not feel its honor. This lone B-17 has the respect of all and teaches that freedom is a job for us all.

21

LETTER TO TERRORISTS

You can kick us, you can hurt us, you can bow us, but you will not—read *will not*—defeat us. I'm going to tell you why.

We are Americans. We produce, we build, we work, we are free, we achieve, we help, and we are united. That's who we are. That's what we do. And because of all of the above, we have given more people a better life and a better standard of living than any country on Earth. We are not better than others—we are simply free. And we are not about to give it up. No way. No how. Never.

You need to know something else: In your vile attack, you didn't just turn a government and its military against you—you turned an entire nation of people against you. And you cannot defeat an entire nation of people. Read that again: You cannot defeat an entire nation of people. Because Americans speak out and disagree in public, you may think we are not united, fractured even. You are wrong. That's actually how we get along. It's how we reach conclusions. We don't dictate. We reach a consensus.

And speaking of being united, I see your people on television, dancing in the streets, burning our flag, chanting anti-American slogans, and waving anti-American signs. If you had uncensored television, here's what you would see in America: states, counties, cities, and people are united like never before. Flags are everywhere—on homes, on cars, and outside businesses. A sign in front of 12th Street Radiator reads "God Bless America," and another at Cascade Storage reads "Honk if You Love America," and another at ABC Printing says "Pray for America." This, all over America! To defeat us you'd have to kill our fiber, our character, our unity, our way of life, and you will never be able to do that.

You are small bands of extremists, scattered, holed-up, hit-and-run cowards. So you will have random, occasional successes (by your sick way of thinking). But you can never win. Our people believe in our economy and our way of life, so to defeat them, you'd have to defeat all of them. You'll never do that because each one of them is doing his or her part for our way of life. From selling groceries, insurance, cars, and fence posts, to building houses, cars, and airplanes, from working in hospitals to teaching in schools—every person doing each of these things is working against you. I say it again to drive the point home: Never will you defeat all of us. Never. And you can take that to the bank.

Here's something else you need to know: We do not hate. You, it seems, are driven by hatred. It drives you to kill, to even kill yourself. There is no future in that. Nor is there any glory in it. It is sick, stupid, and wrong. I'm quite sure I can't change your mind, but I want to emphasize this: Your terrorist ways accomplish nothing, and they will be your undoing.

I said we do not hate. Think about that for a minute. The Gulf War, Somalia, Serbia—remember them? Guess who the United States was defending? Muslims. We defend freedom so people can believe what they will. Read that to mean "tolerance of beliefs."

You, it appears, tolerate nothing outside your own beliefs. Why? How? You are mere mortals, subject to mistaken beliefs. How can you be so sure you are the only correct believers? How arrogant. How wrong.

Want evidence that you are wrong? Not just the United States, but the world is uniting against you. As you wither on the vine, we will grow, be strong, hug and love our children, take care of our elderly, and be a nation who cherishes and defends our way of life. We will prosper; you will not.

Have you ever restored an old car, built wings for an airplane, planted a garden and eaten fresh-shelled peas, planted flowers, or had a summer barbecue with friends? Small, silly things to you perhaps, but these are the things of individual happiness, contentment, and friendship. It's stuff that makes you feel good. It is stuff that makes you want to live and provide more of the same for your family. It is life...as it should be lived. And you? Hatred and killing. Think about it. Your way does no good; it won't work. Never has and never will.

And think about this for a minute: You hurt our economy...temporarily. But what you don't understand is that while you may have hurt one part, you stimulate another. Our flag manufacturers are going gangbusters. We're diverse, and we're free. When one door closes, we open another. That's our way. It's how we've gotten where we are, and it's how we'll stay where we are.

Is your hatred driven by desperation? I ask because I do not understand your hatred. Your not being free is not my fault. Your government may be a dictatorship, but there are ways, with determination, to change that. The founding fathers of America fled oppression to found this nation. And, with great wisdom for which I am thankful, they wrote a document—probably the finest ever written—the Constitution of the United States of America. It guarantees individual freedoms. And we Americans live by it. It works. Magnificently.

Sure, our government speaks for us, our military will throw some bombs and bullets your way—and we are behind them 100 percent—but it is the fiber of our nation that you are at war with, and it is that very fiber that you will not be able to break. We are too united, too diverse, and too free to be defeated.

Look up for a minute. See our land. Have you seen the fall colors of Maine, the wheat fields of Kansas, the cotton of Texas, the apples of Washington state, the Rocky Mountains, the Oregon coast? That's our land—our vistas. Think we're gonna let a few nut cases like you take that from us? Think again because it ain't gonna happen. Amber waves of grain. Home of the brave. Land of the free. That's the United States.

Have I made my point? Give it up. You cannot win. We seek not land. We seek not to change your way of life. We seek not to harm any people. But we will not be trampled by bands of terrorist cowards. We are one nation. Indivisible. Unbowed. Strong. And now, thanks to you, even stronger.

22

COMMUNIST CO-PILOT

Here's a curve ball for you: My co-pilot is a communist. Or he was a communist. The whole thing is rather incongruous to me. Let me see if I can piece it together for you.

I'd heard through the rumor mill at my airline that we'd hired a communist pilot. Huh? Seems as though this new hire was a former member of the Soviet Air Force and flew IL-76s. When the Soviet Union started crumbling, he took the opportunity to defect. It's something he'd had in his mind for some time, but had kept very much to himself. In a country like the Soviet Union, such thoughts are simply not tolerated. Speak your mind there—like we do here—and you're liable to find yourself at the bottom of the Minsk.

While on a stopover, and during a lull in training, our communist simply walked away from his crew—and kept walking. His plan was to reach the East German border before nightfall. He miscalculated, thought he was closer to the border than he was. He stayed off the roads but heard sounds and cars, every one of which, in his mind, was the authorities looking for him. After a couple hours, he *knew* the authorities would be looking for him.

He was still walking when it got dark. He didn't dare use a flashlight. He stumbled along, scared, excited, and full of doubts in a strange country, using the moon for guidance. He came upon what looked like a border, best as he could make it out. He held up short of the border, waiting, watching, wondering, and listening. He was cold but his adrenaline was high.

At dawn he made his break, not knowing what to expect. In his mind all he knew was that it was "now or never." He crossed the border, not knowing if electronic detection devices protected it, and just kept running. And running some more. Where to, he did not know. Just away.

He found refuge in West Germany, but he *still* will not talk about where.

From West Germany he found his way to the United States, where he got a job delivering pizzas to pay for American flying lessons. He said some of his instructors weren't very good, finding out later that a couple of them were FBI agents with private pilot certificates who were just checking....

Here's where you have to get into this with me: In my upbringing, communists had always been the enemy. The big-bad-four-eyed-mean-and-nasty enemy. My Dad always told me they were bad. When my third grade teacher said, "Drop!," we were to dive under our desks to protect ourselves from the bombs the communists were sure to drop on us someday. Then I spent twenty-four years in the military, and for almost all that time the communists were the enemy. No two ways about it, they were bad dudes. It follows that I didn't like them at all.

But now, at this moment, here *was* one, sitting beside me in the cockpit of an airliner in the registry of the United States of America. And there's a whole bunch of people sitting in the back of the airplane counting on us, the two former enemies, to fly safe. Weird? Yeah!

I figured I'd best make some conversation, so for openers I said, "I used to do target study on your house." I can't believe I said that, but I did! He said, "I did the same on yours, colonel." (Someone had *told* him I'd been in the military.) Uneasy glances and head nodding followed this exchange, but it broke the ice.

So what brought us together? That part is easy: We were both just two young boys who wanted to fly airplanes. For me it was routine Americana: go to school, fly a Cessna 150, join the U.S. Air Force, fly jets, get off active duty and fly for the National Guard and an airline, and buy a Champ and fly it anywhere, anytime.

Opportunity abounds in America. Not so for my communist friend. It was get along, go along, pay homage to The Party, and you might get to fly in the military. Initially, homage was more important than aptitude. He played the game and was selected to fly. He was a good soldier. But as the Soviet Union began to crumble, things got worse.

He said they'd fly troops to towns in unrest, and the troops would shoot their own citizens. (The thought just curdles the American mind, doesn't it?) Then the political officer—*always* in tow—told them it was for the good of The Motherland. My friend said it was "total hogwash" (not his exact words...his American slang is quite good). All of which brings us back to the beginning of this story: He made the final decision to defect.

But never mind all that right now: We still had to fly together. I mean, he *looked* like a communist, dark hair, heavy beard, and he spoke with an accent. I worried what would happen at the busy airports when the controller, in one breath, said, "Liner 23, you're 5 miles from LAWTN, turn left heading one-three-zero, maintain 3,000 until intercepting the localizer, you're cleared for the ILS one-six-right approach, maintain at least one-ninety to eight DME, then one-seventy to the outer marker, contact tower there one-one-nine-point-nine."

Guess what? I needn't have worried. He got it. This guy very much wanted to be doing what he was doing; he knew what he had to learn and he learned it. It was impressive.

As good as he is in the airplane, there are still some things he has a tough time comprehending in America. It amazes him that you can walk into a grocery store or a hardware store, and the shelves are full. It amazes him that you can get in a car and drive anywhere. And it totally boggles his mind to think that you can get in a private airplane and fly anywhere. The things we take for granted? He calls them, "Freedom."

He has been able to bring his wife and mother to the United States from Russia. His father is still there, and he'd like to go back and get him but says, "I know the Soviet Union is no more, but I know parts of the KGB still exist. If they found me there, they would kill me." That statement lends new perspective to the idea of freedom, does it not?

My friend is a curiosity to others on the crew, too. One flight attendant asked, "Didn't you, like, drink a lot in the Soviet Union?"

"Yeah, we did," he answers, "but we didn't have anything else to do. Here you can go to a movie, bowl, boat, golf, drive, shop."

My friend will have a beer with you, but he no longer drinks just to drink.

Notice I haven't mentioned his name? He doesn't want it mentioned. There was paranoia where he grew up; mistrust was rampant. He's comfortable in America now, but his makeup remains that you be a little careful about what you say to whom. I can respect that.

As you can probably tell, we've become friends. I still call him a communist, and he calls me a capitalist, but together we often marvel how it is that governments can get so far apart when individual people, at heart, are a lot the same. I do know this: I'm glad to be living in America. How about you?

23

68-C

Like many classes, we came from all across the country: California, New York, Texas, Kansas, Minnesota, Alabama, Arizona. We were reporting for U.S. Air Force Undergraduate Pilot Training (UPT) at Webb Air Force Base, Big Spring, Texas, a small town with a big heart. It was 1966. Vietnam was happening and the country was divided. We were all in our early 20s with 20/20 vision and an eye toward the sky. We badly wanted to be jet pilots, and for the next 53 weeks that would be the sole purpose of our existence (well, almost…the occasional beer and the occasional date—I met my bride of 35 years there). Sixty-three of us signed in; 47 graduated.

I remember the last leg of my trip to Texas. It was from El Paso to Big Spring in my 1966 Volkswagen Beetle. My venerable 1959 Bug gave up en route, blowing smoke and oil all over the road outside San Luis Obispo, California. I needed a new car. I had a checking account, but no credit—didn't know a credit card from an ion—so the local banker called my bank at home, and my banker told him I was "a good kid." A couple hours after breaking down I was on my way again in a new VW without ever filling out a credit application.

Twenty miles outside of Big Spring is the town of Stanton. The sign said, "Welcome to Stanton—home of 3,000 friendly people and a few old soreheads." I thought to myself, I think I'm going to like it here. I like these people already. Outside of Big Spring, its sign read, "Welcome to Big Spring—home of Oil, Cattle, Hospitals, Industry, and Jet Pilots." All right! JET PILOTS. That was what I was here for. I was a day early for check-in, so I stayed at a motel just outside the gate to the base. I didn't sleep a wink. I worked my whole life of twenty-two years to get here, and now, just outside the door, my dream was before me, about to become reality.

We signed in, signed a lot of papers, took physicals, got issued a ton of books, and most importantly, were issued flight suits, helmets, gloves, a cool watch, and even cooler sunglasses. We were designated class 68C, and we took the stuff to our rooms and spread it out and looked at it. Unbelievable! It was happening!

We started out flying the T-41—a subsonic, all-metal, high-wing interceptor that was marketed in other venues as a Cessna 172, though none of us talked about that. Its purpose was to inexpensively determine whether we had the aptitude to fly. Most of us did; some didn't. That's how the game was played.

I remember day one of T-41s. We piled off the bus and stood in formation while Capt. Young inspected us. Hank "Stabes" Stabler, from Arizona, had a haircut that was blocked, instead of tapered, in the back. Totally radical! Young stood behind him and said, "You're in the military now. Get a haircut!" Stabes later flew F-4s, got out, went into school administration, and never flew again. When I finish my RV-8, I'm going to go get him, strap his butt in the back, and show him—once again— the ground through the top of a canopy. He'll weep.

Then it was on to T-37s—an airplane that doesn't get a lot of respect but is just a sweetheart to fly—with P-51 performance but jet smoothness. I remember my first solo in it: I did four loops in a row and came home and wrote in my logbook, "Life's complete."

Then we graduated from the Tweet to the Talon—the T-38— fast, furious, pretty, powerful, and with fingertip response. Along the way, stuff happened, legends were born, nicknames were given, and careers began.

Tommie McLeroy (KC-135), from Heflin, Alabama, once took the active runway in a T-37, solo, "ready" for takeoff, with his canopy wide open. Someone later told his instructor about it, and the response was, "Well, heck, you can't expect 'em to remember everything!"

Phil Miller (F-105) once entered the traffic pattern in a T-37 complaining, "I can't get over 160 knots with 100 percent power." The mobile tower replied, "Roger. Raise your speed brake and re-enter the pattern." His UPT nickname after that? You guessed it: "Speed Brake."

Gerry Veltrie (B-52) logged 1.7 hours in a T-37 that held only 1.3 hours of fuel. Nickname: "Dry Tanks."

Doug Silver (F-4) shut down both engines of a T-38 on a taxiway when one engine was indicating high oil pressure. You can't start a T-38 without external air, so he was "dead in the water." Nickname after that: "Shutdown."

Bruce "Bruiser" Peterson (died in an F-4) held the record for filling barf bags. He had the neatest dry sense of humor and could make anybody laugh. McLeroy once barfed in his glove. He held it tightly but spilled it while getting out of the airplane. His instructor said, "Next time I'm going to make you do it in your helmet."

We had to give our fuel state before requesting a closed pattern (lest we idiot student pilots would run out of fuel having too much fun in the pattern), so John "Snapper" Beal (F-100, F-104, F-4) requested a closed pattern with "615 pounds" fuel. You could barely read the gauges within 100 pounds, so we gave him some guff over that one. Snapper took guff good; he laughs easily.

Gary VanOvermeiren (KC-135) got lost flying a straight-in approach to a practice field. By the time he found the field again, it had closed for the day. Rich "Cas" Castle (T-28, F-4) finished number one in the class. We asked him, "Are you good?" He'd answer, "Sometimes." Actually, we all thought we were good...sometimes.

Along the way, in academics and on the flightline, we were awarded "Dummy Debits" for various mental miscalculations. Get too many Dummy Debits and you got to go to "Dummy Dungeon" in the evenings. It was sort of like a high school study hall. It wasn't too bad, unless it was on a Friday night. Then it was bad.

At year's end we put together an annual. Actually, Charles "Chuck Chad" Chadwick (F-100, F-105) put most of it together, he being "the keeper of the pictures" and a high-energy guy. On the front it says "68C." On a back page I wrote, almost 40 years ago now, this:

What does it all mean—a year of pilot training?

First of all, and outwardly, it means we can wear the wings of Air Force pilots. And proudly we will do so.

More important is what it all means inwardly. It means that flying is a part of our lives...and always will be. It means that airplanes, aerodynamics, navigation, instruments, "grease jobs," and "hangar flying" are all a part of our lives...and always will be.

In the end, too, we are all "tigers," and in our hearts we hope we always will be.

That is what it means, not in entirety, of course, but in a nutshell. We are pilots now and in the future and, most of all, we are damn proud of it.

My question now is to find out if what I wrote those forty years ago is true. Of the classmates I'm still in touch with, it mostly is.

But I've lost track of many of them. (We're going to try to remedy that this year at EAA AirVenture.) Keep in mind that these guys now are nearing 60. Such is life. But they still think they're good...sometimes. But does flying still burn within? Are they still good at that? That is the question.

Snapper retired from the Air Force and now does something regarding "military deployments" for the government. He owns a Cessna Cardinal. Cas also retired from the Air Force and now is a "high mucky-muck" with Mesa Pilot Development. Chuck Chad owns a landscaping business and flies a Pitts in aerobatic competitions. Speed Brake retired from the Air Force and runs a successful real estate business.

Stabes retired from school administration but is going to get reacquainted with flying soon. His dad told me at graduation, "Heck, I never thought the boy was gonna learn to drive a tractor, let alone an airplane. "Oz" (that's me—KC-135, OV-1) retired from the Guard, will soon retire from an airline, writes for the world's greatest aviation magazine—this one—and is building an RV-8. Most of these guys still have some "tiger" left in them.

Some of the guys I've only heard about here and there. I heard Stan Marks was flying for American. Or was that David Mitchell? Heard Don "Pito" Peterson became a general. Heard Steve "Time Hack" Meltzer flew C-130s for the Guard. Ditto for Don "Basket" Schwab. Flying was, and maybe still is, a part of these guys' lives.

But what of Tommie McLeroy of T-37 canopy fame? Don't know. Or Sam Hodnutt (F-100) from the backwoods of Tennessee? Or John "JL" Long (F-111), the "Beer Call Champion"? Or Bill Looke (F-4), the "Dummy Debit Champion"? Or Jim "Gurk" McGuirk (KC-135), who joined ROTC so he wouldn't have to take PE in college? Or John "Foghorn" Mickley (KC-135)? Or Noidrie Moses from the Citadel? Or Shutdown? Or Dry Tanks? I dunno! Are these guys still flying? Interested in flying? My survey is incomplete and my question unanswered until I hear from them and all the rest.

But here's my hunch: Many are still flying. Many are still interested. A few aren't. But I do know that the fire once burned in all of them, and they're proud of that. And they'll all talk about that. And, in their minds, they're still "tigers." After all, once a proud pilot, always a proud pilot. So, in that sense, what I wrote those many years ago is true. But the study continues, so here's the deal: On a day to be determined, about mid-AirVenture 2004, we're going to meet at the base of the control tower at OSH (three of us did last year), shake hands, tell lies, and go from there. If I've found any of you with this column and you're interested, contact me so we can begin connecting the dots that were once U.S. Air Force UPT class 68C. Are you still out there? Flying?

So.....if you see a bunch of "mature looking" guys gathered at the base of the tower at OSH, all talking with their hands, squinting to recognize the person standing next to them, listening to Chuck Chad talking about his "hairy F-100 mission in Nam" or about pruning roses, stop by. Pilot talk is universal. We all love a story, whether it's from class 44G or 68C. We all still love flying. That's my hunch, and I'm sticking to it.

24

AN AIRPLANE LOVED

It was an unlikely airplane to become attached to. It was rather a subtle seduction. We used to call it "Grumman ugly." It had a big nose-- in the mold of an A-6 --tapering to a wasp-like end attached to triple tails. My bride used to call it "the bug-eyed cigar." But it was always a hit at airshows because it had so many angles. It was eye-catching in its ugliness. And therein lay its beauty: It was about function. All about function. There was not a frivolous bone in its body. It was built for the mission-- tactical reconnaissance and surveillance --and only the mission. And it was a dang lotta fun.

I'm talking about the Grumman OV-1D "Mohawk." I flew it for sixteen years with the Oregon National Guard and I enjoyed every hour I ever flew it. I flew one type airliner for eight years. That is the closest competition as far as my longevity with one airplane. I've never been one to make a big deal about different type airplanes flown. I'd rather fly one well for a long time than fly a hundred different types briefly. That's just my airplane personality. I always said that you never really know an airplane until you've flown it through all the seasons. After sixteen years, I knew every sight, sound, smell, feel and nuance of the Mohawk. And I grew to love them all.

You know where I'm going with this, don't you? Some airplanes just get under your skin and crawl their way to your heart and grab you. That's not a bad thing.

The OV-1-- I flew the B, the C, the Super-C, and the D, all upgrades in avionics, wings or engines --was single pilot, with stick, ejection seat and a great mission. It don't hardly get no better'n that! The other crewmember operated the surveillance gear, conventional camera, infrared camera or the radar. He/she had no flight controls. They were a trusting lot.

The flying day always started with a bit of ritual. You got a mission briefing-- your target or targets --and filed a flight plan then went to your locker. It was a tall metal locker with your name on it: PAINE. Down the row were the names of other pilots: POLANSKY, KAUFFMAN, BURNS, COPE, RUX, DWYER, HAMMONS, DEGNER. The locker had a combination lock on it. I don't remember the combination today but I do remember the clang and rattle of the door as it opened and revealed your helmet, oxygen mask, ejection seat harness, survival vest, "water wings" (if going over water), and kneeboard with checklist and mission equipment information. You threw your harness and vest over your shoulder, grabbed your helmet and kneeboard and began the walk to your steed. The anticipation was grand.

At the airplane, the ritual continued. You hung your harness and vest on a drop tank hard-point and put your helmet up in the seat. The crew chief usually had all the safety pins laid out for you, the gear pins, drop tank safety pins and the ejection seat pins. There were seven safety pins attached to a red lanyard for each ejection seat. The crew chief folded the lanyard so you could count the pins. You counted seven pins....always. The observer was busy 'running-up' the mission equipment and navigational gear (in the early years, Doppler, and later the INS (Inertial Navigation System)). They got very good at it. When you were finding a dark target at night below the hilltops, lives depended on the accuracy of the equipment.

During the preflight you knew you were readying a thoroughbred. Everything you touched was solid "Grumman Iron." Climbing on top of the airplane you could check the main fuel tank quantity visually. Standard external fuel configuration was two 150 gallon drop tanks-- full for the longer radar missions and 50 gallons a side for shorter missions. You could slap the tanks with your hand and confirm which load you had.

Climbing aboard was also a ritual because it had to be done right. You strapped on your ejection seat harness-- tight! --and vest then pushed the little flap on the upper step that pushed the lever that released the lower step. Right foot on lower step, left foot on upper step, right knee on the seat-- pause to check the upper and lower firing handles on the ejection seat were in the safe position --left foot on the floor, pull yourself up via the glare shield hand-hold then right foot on the floor and settle into your very busy, very cozy duty station. Then listen for the crew chief to slam the lower step back up into the stowed and locked position. TDU (Threat Display Unit) on the left....so you could know if the bad guys were tracking you on radar. Start, fuel, lights and electrics on the overhead, "eyebrow" panel. Engine instruments on the right, and throttles, gear, flaps, speed brake, emergency drop tank and emergency gear release center. Continuing down center and right were the mission equipment control heads and every kind of radio known to mankind, FM (for talking to the troops), VHF, UHF, and HF (for talking to HQ) and nav radios ADF, VOR, TACAN and the aforementioned INS. You could select any of the nav radios to be displayed on one RMI needle. We called that the suicide panel. You *had* to know what the needle was pointing to before you used it. The flight instruments-- round dials, if I need to say so -- were, of course, right in front of you and the stick was in your.....left hand. That's unusual for a military airplane but after a bit it became second nature.

The Martin-Baker ejection seat had very little cushion. It was hard by design (better on the spine during an ejection). Ours was a sixty-knot seat, meaning you had to have sixty knots forward velocity in order to be able to eject successfully on the ground. The chute was in the seat so you merely strapped yourself in with the leg garters, seat belt (part of your harness) and parachute riser/shoulder harness. If you had to eject, pull the upper or lower firing handle and you'd be hanging under a chute in short order. Release the seat pack survival kit you were sitting on and before you knew it-- plunk! --you were on the ground. Nice to have…never had to use it. To this day I have one vertebra that is slightly enlarged because it's the one that rested on the ejection seat back when I was flying. I'd wiggle around but it would always come back to that same bone. If I flew several days in a row, it would hurt. It was a pain I was willing to endure. Also, to this day, I always feel better in an airplane if I'm a little uncomfortable. I can't explain why. And I don't like too much frough-frough in an airplane. I like function. Look in the cockpit of my RV-8 this summer at AirVenture and you'll see what I mean. My sixteen years in the OV-1 imprinted me.

The flying? It almost goes without saying, doesn't it? How an airplane so ugly could fly so well, I'll never know. But it did. You could impose your will on it at the flick of a wrist. It was made to comply. Lowering the flaps automatically extended an extra set of ailerons, the inboards, to the twenty-five degree down position, where they became flaperons. You could stand the airplane on a wingtip and turn on a dime. Forward visibility was not great but with the bulbous side window you could see out and straight down unrestricted.

Mission wise, with conventional cameras you had to fly right over the target. You could mount a flasher pod for night but we always said that just gave the enemy gunners a good lead to shoot at. We usually used the infrared camera at night. It was passive but you still had to fly right over the target. Late night, lights out, below the ridge tops, relying on the INS for position-- it could be a little dicey. But if that's what the mission called for, that's what you did. "Get in and get out" was the name of the game.

The airplane's mission forte was the SLAR (Side Looking Airborne Radar). You could stand-off and fly in friendly territory and still "see" far behind the enemy line. You could data link that info to a ground commander or even call in more urgent targets. The ground troops loved it. Strategic reconnaissance, i.e., satellites, eventually took over the mission but ground commanders lost the immediacy they had with us. Improved technology is not always an improvement.

Even in the stand-off SLAR mode, we were still vulnerable to certain types of missiles. But that just went with the territory. I can remember being in international waters using the SLAR to look at the port of a foreign country suspected of smuggling arms and my TDU was chirping, telling me that I was being tracked. Then it went solid line/solid tone to indicate a lock. All I could think was, 'If you hurt my airplane, I'm going to be really, really angry.' That must have scared them off because they never fired.

I loved the overhead pattern in the Mohawk. You'd fly up 'initial' at 1500' AGL at 220 knots, bank sharply and yank and "pop the boards" (speedbrakes) right over the approach end of the runway. At the 180 degree point you'd drop gear, full flaps, begin your descent and stay in your sixty degrees of bank until just before touchdown on the numbers. Fun? Oh golly my golly yes.

I remember one calm, clear night. I was alone in the airplane and alone in the pattern. I couldn't stop doing what I was doing. I'd takeoff, pull up, lead the level off by about three hundred feet, roll into a ninety degree bank and the nose would drop and I'd roll out at pattern altitude on the crosswind. Then I'd fly out for another 'initial.' I did that fifteen times. The crew chief on duty that night told me, "The first two times you landed, I walked out to your parking place to wave you in. Later I waited until I saw you coming into the ramp area." I told him, "I got raptured." For the next ten years, every time I flew at night and that crew chief was on duty he'd ask me, "You're not going to get raptured, are you?"

And I remember my last overhead pattern, sixteen years after I first flew the OV-1. I called, "Scan 14, three mile initial for the approach end left break." And my voice broke! I was emotional. Here I was, ensconced in the busy, cozy cockpit I had grown to love, feeling, hearing, sensing everything......for the last time! "Left break approved, cleared to land," replied the tower. The tower knew the moment; they'd read about the unit's mission change in the news.

Over the numbers now, brisk left bank, the sky blurs, slight power reduction, by the wrist and by the sound, speed brake out and pull, feeling the G's. They feel good, like they always have. Try to remember the sound, the feel, the motion. The airplane's in real-time; my mind's in slow motion. Lower the gear, hear and feel the clunk, lower the flaps to full, re-trim about three flicks of the trim and settle into 120 knots around the corner. I don't want this to end. Still in sixty degrees of bank, descending. Why do things have to end? I'm bringing my airplane home; my airplane's bringing me home....like it always has. I've lost four engines in my career, two of them in the OV-1. It still brought me home. Runway's coming into view. Still sixty degrees of bank. I love this airplane. Runway centerline's becoming center, full length in view now. Couple hundred more feet to earth. Time to be gentle. One steady, easy motion to wings level and a gentle thunk-thunk and we're on the ground-- the stupid ground! --and rolling. Hold the nose high, proud-like. As the speed decreases, lower the nose gracefully and pull the props into reverse slowly, not because you need the reverse but because you love the sound-- woosh! The sound punctuates the end of the flight, in this case, the end of an era.

I taxi to my parking spot. I know that when the crew chief crosses her arms over her head to stop me that she feels the emotion, too. I don't immediately shut down the engines; I want to hear them just a little longer. Then, almost instinctively and without looking, I reach over and move the right lever to 'fuel shutoff.' The right engine winds down. We're still half alive. Then I look at the left prop while I pull the left lever to 'fuel shutoff.' The noise changes and the prop begins winding down. I don't remember anything after that.

Silly? Only if you've never loved an airplane.

Years later, I'm healed now. But I can mentally take myself back to a steep bank, high-G overhead pattern in a heartbeat. And I often do. I've loved one airplane and one woman for a long time. I'm a lucky guy.

25

AIRLINE RETIREMENT

I joked with my wife that I was going to call in sick for my last airline trip. That way I could just trudge off into the sunset, no muss, no fuss. She said, "No, you're not." Wives have great wisdom in such matters. And I wasn't going to write about it, either. Too b-o-r-i-n-g.

But I reported for duty as ordered, and flew. Figuratively speaking, it was quite a ride—more emotional than I thought it would be. Several of my fellow airline types, already retired by the foolish age-60 rule, had warned me of the roller coaster emotions I would experience. They were right. So I'll share, because many will follow me.

Actually, I had two "final flights." And my bride of 35 years also retired the same week, so all in all it was quite a journey.

The first "final flight" was on Wednesday, so the proper airline mucky-mucks could be there—as well as the many people in low places that I hang out with. The day started with a motel 0430 wake-up call. (Those I will not miss.) We flew from Fresno, California, to Seattle, Washington, and back to Fresno. The final leg was to be from Fresno to Portland, Oregon.

Two weeks previous, on the same trip, a Fed met us before the last leg and found four screws missing from an access panel that has 65 screws. He grounded us, and we ended up ferrying the airplane back to Portland. This time we were ready for him. Jay, my capable first officer, counted all the exterior screws on the airplane, all 27,842,729 of them, and they were all there. (A person can become a little "flip" when a person is about to retire.) But the guy didn't show up.

So we flew our final leg from Fresno to Portland as scheduled.

The cat was out of the bag, because every controller said, "Congratulations." That was a nice touch. These are the people I've talked to nearly every day for twenty-six years but never met. I wanted to say something cute, like, "Thanks for separating me," but I didn't. I just said, "Thank you very much."

On final into Portland, I could see the fire trucks stationed at exit Bravo Five. I thought, "No way I'm going to make that exit without slamming the passenger's heads into the seat back in front of them."

So I turned off at my usual exit for Runway 28L, Bravo Four, and got very explicit instructions from ground control to "turn right on Bravo, join the ramp at Bravo Five, and taxi to the gate." At Bravo Five, the fire trucks gave us the traditional spray job. I said to Jay, "I hope they don't flame us out." They didn't. I waved a "thank you" to them. It was just pretty darn neat!

As I taxied up to the gate I could see a bunch of people standing there. But most of all I could see my wife and youngest son flashing me a thumbs-up. I liked that a lot. Every passenger getting off the airplane shook my hand and said, "Congratulations." I liked that, too.

Then my wife and son came to the cockpit; we hugged and then walked to the reception through a group of clapping friends. I kept thinking, "Okay, you people, stop being so nice. I don't want to be emotional." At the reception I was able to tell a few stories and lies, and that got me comfortable again. My wife spoke, too, saying, "When I started dating him as a young pilot, I never thought of sleeping with him as a grandfather." She was fun to be with when we were dating, and she's still fun to be with.

The company gave me a framed collage of all the types of airliners I had flown and a model of the most recent one flown. After cake and soft drinks—and yet more stories and lies—I turned in the trip paperwork, and we were off to the parking lot. I was wrung out.

On Friday my wife retired. She's an RN and has worked at the same busy medical practice for twenty-two years. Being the caring, Texas-raised girl she is, she has hundreds of patients who love her—and they all came to her reception. I've never seen one person get so many hugs! I stood in a corner and watched, proud. Caring people in medicine really do touch lives.

Then on Saturday, I had my final flight from Portland to Los Angeles and back. This time no festivities were planned, but I got to have my family and friends on board. A fun time was had by all. We were an hour late—a fitting end to an airline career—but no one seemed to mind. All the deplaning passengers spoke and shook my hand again. I was beginning to like the concept.

For my final flight I chose Gabe as my first officer. He's a story unto himself, and I admire him a lot. Raised in Ethiopia, he learned to fly there. Then a different government took over the country, and he was forced to leave. (That's a difficult concept for the American mind to grasp, isn't it?)

Gabe then came to America and scratched-and-clawed and worked his way up the aviation ladder to the right seat of an airliner. He asked for nothing; he earned everything. See why I admire him? He and his wife recently bought their first house. He says they sit in it with their daughter and say, "I can't believe this is ours!" He is now putting in a yard and is planting grass for the first time in his life. The guy has a perpetual smile on his face and will readily tell anyone, "This is a great country." Next time you hear somebody whining about not having this or that, tell 'em about Gabe.

I wish I could say my final landing was by grand design or skill, but it wasn't. Through mostly luck, it was a roller. As we settled on the struts, I could see Gabe out of the corner of my eye raise his hands and exclaim, "A greaser!" I could also hear the passengers clapping. My wife said later, "I could feel you working for that one." And to my pilot buddies who are saying, "Yeah, but you probably touched down 3,000 feet down the runway," I'll only admit to it being 2,000 feet down, but hey, I still had 6,000 feet in front of me.

After that final flight, we all got off the airplane, Gabe moved up a seniority number, I turned in the paperwork (again), we all went out for adult beverages and fine dining, and we talked the night away.

The next day we met up with our son the Marine, his wife, and our grandson, who had just arrived from the East Coast on leave between duty stations. So, from final flight to family, it simply felt like we were on vacation. I was playing "horsy" and "wagon puller" with my grandson and my back and knees hurt, but I never felt better. Like I said, on vacation.

But this past weekend, our kids went to the other in-laws for four days. After that, they'll return, and we'll accompany them to Camp Pendleton, California, and help them settle into their new assignment, prior to our son's deployment. So, for the first time since all this began, we had quiet time. In one evening lull my wife said, "I'm proud of you." I said to her, "I'm proud of you, too." We were both wrung out, but in retrospect, it was well worth the ride.

Now on the agenda is EAA AirVenture in July, which may be over by the time you read this. That's the perfect lead-in to our next life: flying, writing, friends, and travel.

I'm going to finish the RV-8—now my full-time job—and maybe even get it on the cover of a magazine. And I want to meet the people I've met through this column, readers who stay in touch and whom I know are special people in character. I want to meet Jack, a World War II vet in New York; Verne, another World War II vet from Washington; and Dave, an energetic spokesman for general aviation in California.

I've met Tom from Texas (who confirmed my hunch about good people), but I also want to meet his friend, George, who wrote, "Flying airliners is what I did, not who I was." And I want to fly to a zillion small airports and meet the guy sitting in the chair at the line shack. And I want to meet you there, too.

Retirement for real, however, sort of sank in this past Monday morning. I was on my hands and knees with a can of white paint and a small paintbrush, touching up the interior baseboards of the house from years of furniture strikes. That's a job I had managed to put off for 20 years. Now I was doing it. That's retirement.

But here's the *coup de grace*. Because I didn't want to miss a minute of my son's military leave home, I retired a month early. It was my way of saying to the Feds, "You can't fire me. I quit!" It was a small leap for mankind, but a giant leap for this pilot. (You pilots understand.) Truth be known, the fun and flying are just beginning.

26

SEAT'S OPEN

I recently helped a young man get hired at my airline. Getting hired by an airline is a fickle adventure, especially given the state of the industry today. It used to be that you just wanted to get hired by any airline. No longer. Now you want to get hired by a solvent airline and the competition remains keen for those jobs. Separating yourself from the pack with but a piece of paper called a resume is difficult. So it helps when you get a personal recommendation from someone who worked at the airline for twenty-six years (before getting the Feds' age sixty ax) and who knows the chief pilots personally. That would be me.

Mark is a friend of my youngest son so I had met him and observed his aviation progress. He is a clean-cut, hard working kid, which is one of the reasons I chose to recommend him. He got the required ratings, flight instructed and flew charter. But multi-engine time and actual instrument time comes slow in that environment. I told him, "Fly freight in a light twin in the winter." So he did. It was then that I called my friends at the airline and got his resume moved to the top of the stack. He got the interview, got the job, worked his fanny off and is now flying the line. Mark writes me how grateful he is for my help. I tell him, "I helped you get your foot in the door. You did the rest."

But, of course, there's more to this story. From a long time ago.

I still remember his face. Not just his face, but the look on it. I did not, however, fully appreciate it at the time. I was young, in my twenties. He was old (or so I thought), probably in his late forties or early fifties. I was the co-pilot. He was the pilot. The aircraft was a KC-135 and we had just landed after his last flight. His retirement was two days away.

His name was Col. Saunders. I don't remember his first name. Colonels didn't have first names in those days; he was just Col. Saunders, grey hair, stocky, smoked a pipe. We were a crew of four: I was young, the navigator was young and the boom operator was young. They called us "Col. Saunders and his Mod-Squad." He just chuckled and went about his business of being the consummate professional. Nothing much rattled him. Whatever happened, he just worked his way through it. All of us young punks used to marvel at that. We also, I think, learned from it.

Perhaps Col. Saunders' calm came from flying combat missions in B-24's in WWII. Which he did. Or from getting shot up over Ploesti. Which he did. Or from having a hung-over co-pilot pass out on him during a combat mission in the B-24 and stay passed out until the mission was over. Which happened to him. Or from the myriad of other experiences he'd had during his thirty-some-odd years of service in the Air Force. Whatever, he was always the calm in the storm.

He had emotion, it's just that you didn't see it very often. I saw it on his last flight. It was a pretty routine mission. We flight planned, filed, pre-flighted, took off, aerial refueled somebody, somewhere (I don't remember), went around a couple thunderstorms and winged our way home to Dyess AFB, Texas. I don't even remember the type of approach we flew but I do remember it was a nice day with deep blue skies and some puffy, scattered clouds. And I remember this: I looked over at Col. Saunders on short final and it finally occurred to my short term young brain that this was this guy's last flight. 'Hmmmmm,' I thought to myself, 'wonder what that's like?' Then that thought went away followed by, 'Shoot! That's eons away for me.'

I continued to watch Col. Saunders. The KC-135 (Boeing 707) is a pretty big airplane but Col. Saunder's control movements were deft, positive, and just right. His gaze moved from inside to outside, from outside to inside, as he continued with a nudge here and there on the controls and then, in the flare, he moved the throttles slowly back, back a little more, then all the way back and the big airplane rolled onto the runway, put there by the ol' Zen Master. Not much was said during the taxi in. Nor even during the parking and shutdown. It didn't have to be.

And then it happened. And it's still seared in my memory. Remember when I told you I remembered his face? Here's what I remember: As the engines wound down I looked over at Col. Saunders and here was this crusty but gentle veteran looking back at me with.........red eyes full of tears. Damn! And then he said, "Seat's open," unstrapped, got out of the seat, climbed down the ladder and walked across the ramp. The "Mod Squad" was left looking at each other and thinking, "So that's what it's like."

The following weekend, Col. Saunders invited the "Mod Squad' to go boating with him. I remember that, too. We met him at the lake. He had a cabin cruiser-type boat, with a captain's chair and a big nautical steering wheel. He was sitting in the chair, wheel in hand, cruising the lake, grey hair blowing in the breeze, puffing on his pipe and with a great big smile on his face. He was at peace. He'd certainly earned it.

Over the years, I lost track of Col. Saunders. But the memories of him are still fresh.

Well, guess what? Eons turned into the blink of an eye and it was me making my last airline flight. On that day Col. Saunders crossed my mind. In a sense, my helping Mark get hired was my way of saying, "Seat's open." And so, someday, Mark will do the same for someone else and the cycle will continue. And that, as they say, is a good thing.

27

HANGAR VISIT

I arrived at the hangar early. There were some things I wanted to prepare before their arrival. I wanted to have a .032 skin to cleco to a rib and a couple pieces of scrap aluminum ready to rivet. 'Demonstration pieces,' so to speak. Plus, I had my VHF handheld out and tuned to the ATIS frequency. I wanted them to hear that, too. I had already pushed my RV-8 out in front of the hangar. It was shining in the sun. (I always steal extra glances when it's shining in the sun.) I was ready. Or so I thought. At least I was as ready as I could be, considering what was about to happen.

I saw them pull in the parking lot across from my hangar, several Suburban's, Explorer's and mini-vans. I ducked back into the hangar to check my preparations. When I looked out again, here they came. There must have been nineteen or twenty of them-- difficult to count when they're all veering hither and yon. But that's what you do when you're five years old. Behind the ragged gaggle of hopping, skipping, happy innocents were their teacher and some parents. Ahhh, good! I can barely keep order with my two grandsons, let alone twenty bouncing boys and girls.

Their teacher, Mrs. Gladow, was young but so very good with the kids. But here's what also hit me: I knew Mrs. Gladow, aka Kathy, when *she* was five years old! She and my youngest son were in kindergarten and grade school together. And she married one of my son's best friends. I served in the National Guard with her Dad. It was all a strong reminder that time marches on.

A few months earlier, at a Christmas party, Kathy asked if she might someday bring her class to see my airplane. "Of course," I said. It was a party; I was "relaxed." Well, that was then and this was now: they were here, in my hangar, a whirling dervish of energy. But it was impossible not to be touched by their bright eyes looking up and around, so eager, so pure, so happy, and so full of life. In thirty-five years I'll be ancient or gone and they'll be running the world. I wish them well.

Back to the visit. Mrs. Gladow gathered them-- as best you can gather five year olds --and had them sit on the hangar floor (it's clean) in front of my workbench. The adults gathered behind them, standing. One little girl said, "It smells like gas in here." A little boy looked at her and said, "It's a shop!" I stayed out of it. Kathy then told them to, "Put your listening ears on." With that they all grabbed their ear lobes and looked up at me. I was a little taken aback by that. The Airport Bums that frequent my hangar don't usually put their 'listening ears' on. I thought it was a good idea, though, and made a mental note to try it on them the next time they wandered in the hangar. I then mumbled something like, "Got your listening ears on?" They looked at me like, 'I'm holding my ear lobes, aren't I? What are ya, stupid or something?' The thought flashed through my mind, 'Don't mess with these kids. They're smarter than you are.'

I then pointed to the control tower. "See that big, tall building? That's the control tower. They tell airplanes when they can takeoff and land. Here's what they sound like." With that I turned on the ATIS. When the ATIS said "visibility ten," one little boy yelled out, "Ten!" That started it. Every time they heard a number, they all repeated it. Temperature…."Twelve!" Dew point…..."Eight!" Wind ….."Five!" Then the big numbers, the runway's in use… ."Three-one!" and "Three-four!" The crescendo built until I turned the ATIS off. These kids were good listeners. They listen better than most pilots I know. Must be the 'listening ears' thing.

It was time to talk about building an airplane. I asked the kids how old they were. They raised their hands, some showing five fingers and some showing four. I told them, "You're five years old. It took me seven years to build my airplane, longer than you've been here." That subtlety was pretty much lost on them when their collective looks said, 'So?????' I was saved by one little girl who still had her hands up. She was holding up four fingers on one hand and two fingers on the other hand were going up and down. I looked at her. She was cuter than a week old kitten. She said, "I'm foh ana hafffff!" I coulda hugged her.

It was time to move to the center piece of my presentation: the cleco. Yeah, the cleco! I held one up and asked, "What's this?" I got blank stares; I expected blank stares. I explained, "It's a cleco." I asked again, "What's this?" Four or five of the kids said, "Cleco." I put it behind my back and brought it out again, "What's this?" This time about ten kids said, "Cleco." I then fastened two pieces of aluminum together with the cleco and said, "This is what clecoes do. They hold stuff together." I then held up another cleco and asked, "What's this?" I got twenty small voices in imperfect harmony but excellent volume saying, "Cleco!" I then told them, "When you go home today and your parents ask you what you learned, say 'cleco'. And when you get a new puppy or kitty, I want you to name it Cleco." I then gave Mrs. Galdow a cleco to put in her desk back at school. I was on a roll; it was my only roll.

I then held up a rivet. An itty-bitty 3-3.5 rivet. They said, "I can't see it!" I held it in the palm of my hand for all to see but quickly deduced that something that small that doesn't move or have legs is not going to hold their interest for more than a nano-second. I deduced right. So I put two pieces of aluminum together with a cleco-- this eliciting an uncommanded chorus of "Cleco!" --then put a rivet in the hole next to the cleco. I then put a rivet squeezer on the rivet and squeezed it. (I had already calculated that the noise of my compressor and rivet gun and bucking bar setting a rivet would have scattered my audience into the next county-- not good.) I then removed the cleco and said, "Rivets are what hold these two pieces of aluminum and my airplane together. There are about twelve-thousand rivets holding my airplane together." Mrs. Gladow looked at her class and explained, "That's a big number." I think they were a little under whelmed with all the rivet stuff. I had them at cleco.

It was time to tour the airplane. I started at the front with, "This is a propeller. It pulls the airplane through the air. This is the motor. It's the most expensive part of the airplane."

The questions started with, "Does it cost more than an X-Box?"

I didn't know what an "X-Box" was but *nothing* is more expensive than aircraft engines so I answered, "Yes." I hope I didn't lead the kid astray.

It was then that I lost control of my audience. The line became more of a swarm around the airplane. I circulated within the swarm to answer more questions. There were the usual "how fast" and "how high" questions. And there was one, "Where are the guns?" And one coached (I saw the parent whispering in the child's ear) question, "Where do you put your lug…lug…age?" I showed him the space behind the back seat. Then, pointing to the tail, a little girl asked "What do these numbers (N214KT) mean?" I explained, "Two kids, '14' was my call sign in the National Guard and 'KT' is for Katie, my bride's name." The next question was, "What do these big letters (KLP, on the side of the fuselage) say?" I said, "Those are my bride's initials, for Kay Lyn Paine."

"Why does she have two names?"

"Because in Texas, where she grew up, she's Kay Lyn. Up north, here in Oregon, she's Katie."

"But why?"

"I don't know. Ask Mrs. Gladow."

And I got, "Is your dog named Cleco?"

"Ah, no. We don't have a dog. We have a cat. Her name is Snickers."

I had mentioned earlier, while talking to the kids in the hangar, that my bride and I had flown the airplane to Oshkosh, Wisconsin. Mrs. Gladow explained to the kids for me again, "That's far." A parent standing nearby leaned toward me and said, "Your bride is brave." Another parent came up to me and said, "I used to fly with my Dad when I was a child. I loved it and he loved it. He passed away last week." The stuff of life.

About that time, totally unplanned and unscheduled, a Cherokee taxied around the corner from the hangar beside me. The kids, of course, zeroed in on it and waved. The Cherokee pilot, startled at first, waved back. What pilot doesn't like an audience? And with that my program/presentation was over. The kids all gathered beside my airplane for a picture. Shiny, happy faces with visions of clecos dancing in their heads. Or something like that.

Something kinda odd happened during the kid's visit. It was a subtle happening but it *was* noticeable to me: the regular visiting Airport Bums were no where to be seen! But they *saw*. They just laid low for a bit. They're like that sometimes. Not often, but sometimes. But after the kids left, Tom, my hangar neighbor two hangars down, came over and said, "Wow! My wife's a kindergarten teacher and she says a kid's attention span is equal to his/her age."

I asked, "In minutes or seconds?"

He said, "In minutes."

I said, "Now you tell me!" Whatever, the Airport Bums, though sometimes shy, are big softies, every one of them. They like little kids at airports, too.

Upon reflection, I probably got more out of the visit than the kids did. They got to say "cleco" and see and touch an airplane and maybe, sometime, somewhere, that will spark something in them. I hope so. But I got to meet with young kids and young parents- two of the most important segments in our society. That's good for the heart. A hangar full of kids makes for a good day, even if some of them are only "foh ana hafffff."

28

MAYOR OF HANGAR ROW 34

That's what I called him: The Mayor of Hangar Row 34. I called him that because he was always there. My hangar is 3411. His was 3408—two doors down. And, being retired, that's where "Mayor Bill" spent a lot of his time. He was a fixture. And he always had a smile and a quip. His obituary read, "...He was a popular member of the airport community." Yeah, he was all of that. For sure. But, of course, there's a lot more to the story.

Bill did a lot of things in his 73 years. Bill and his sister operated Lebold's Ice Cream Store when his father could no longer do so. He served in the U.S. Coast Guard. He'd been a meat cutter and an independent trucker, worked in the woods building logging roads, and owned a seafood restaurant called The Blue Whale. He raised two sons, both now married and with children. It's said that variety is the spice of life. I think that's true because Bill knew a lot of things and could talk about a lot of things.

But flying was his passion. He learned to fly as a teenager and owned a succession of small airplanes. He flew all through the years for one reason: he loved it. It was never his profession, but it was always his passion. His last airplane was a Cessna 180. It's still sitting in Hangar 3408. Nose up, proud—and missing Bill.

When Bill began having health problems, he had to have knee surgery. That frustrated him a lot because a 180 is no airplane to be flying with a bum knee. But when his knee was well, he could practically make that airplane talk. He loved the airplane, and it showed in the way he flew it—with care, grace, class, and skill.

Bill would usually stop by my hangar on the way to his airplane, asking the question homebuilders hear a lot: "That airplane done yet?" I'd always answer, "Next week." If he didn't stop by, he'd just roll down the window on his truck, wave as he drove by, and holler, "Next week?" I'd look up and holler back, "Yup!"

During work breaks I'd often wander down to his hangar. There was usually always somebody else there, sitting on the furniture of kitchens and living rooms past. I'd walk up and say, "Doesn't appear to be much work getting done here." Bill always gave the same reply, "Ain't supposed to be."

Under where Bill's hangar "furniture" was arrayed, there was a piece of carpet, obviously from some long ago home. It was not what you'd call pristine. I once asked him, "You change the oil on this carpet, or what?" He said, "Maybe. But, ya see, when the grass blows under the door it sticks to the oil spots and doesn't scatter all over the hangar." Always thinking, that Bill! But my comment must have registered a little deeper than I thought, because one day he came tearing around the corner and screeched to a halt in front of my hangar, leaned out the window of his truck and, proud as heck, yelled, "Hey! I vacuumed my carpet!"

Now *that*, I surmised, was cause for celebration, so I trundled on down to his hangar, sat in the old lawn chair (with the structurally suspect webbing) on the newly "cleaned" carpet, and we proceeded to identify and solve a bunch of the problems of city and county government. We pretty much concluded that if they'd only listen to us, they'd be a heck of a lot better off. They could thank us later, but for now, we just wanted them to know that "we're here for them." I mean, what better place to solve the world's problems than in an airplane hangar with your buddies. Especially after the carpet's been vacuumed.

At our airport we're required to keep the grass mowed around our hangars. I have a small John Deere lawn tractor that I bought new 16 years ago. All I've ever done to it is change the oil and put gas in it. I love my John Deere. And Bill coveted my tractor. So, once in a while, after I'd mowed my grass, I'd mosey down and mow his grass. I mean, what the heck, I *like* to drive my tractor and mow. And he'd always swing by afterward and say, "Hey, thanks!"

Last week, after Bill's passing, I noticed the grass in front of his hangar was getting a little tall. So John Deere and I went down there and mowed it. It probably sounds a little corny, but that mowing was sort of my memorial to Bill. As I went round and round, each time I mowed toward Hangar 3408, I thought of Bill...and of the camaraderie, conversations, friendships, and fun that Bill made happen there. And somehow, someway, I heard him say, "Hey, thanks!"

But something was missing: Bill and something else. His hangar signs! He'd hung two signs on the front sliding door. One read, "Airplane Pilot on Duty." The other read, "Wanted: Good woman. Must have airplane. Send picture of airplane." Politically correct? Probably not. But could Bill pull it off? Yup. But I noticed as I mowed that the signs were gone. The void seemed bigger than the space the two small signs occupied. But that's how life works, isn't it? Things change. I do hope somebody's saving the signs, however. They were...well...so...Bill. But, you know, he really didn't need the second sign any more. He married Mary Ann 30 days before he passed on.

I go back to Bill's obituary: "Bill was a popular member of the airport community and enjoyed countless hours 'hangar flying' and many, many more hours actually flying." Now, you know what? That is a wonderful, I say again, wonderful legacy. Maybe you have to be a pilot or involved in aviation to really understand what I'm saying, but it just is. And it got me to thinking of the other "Mayor Bills" at other hangars at other small airports all across this great land. They're out there, and you gotta love 'em! They are a part of our aviation culture, and without them we'd be just another industry devoid of personality and passion.

Aviation is an apprenticeship, and it's also rich in its legacies. When you give yourself to aviation, you give yourself to a long line of characters, dreamers, doers, and fond memories. And there's something else: You're not forgotten in aviation. You're just not. Again, maybe you have to be in aviation to really understand that. But Hangar 3408 will always be where Bill held court and kept his Cessna 180. No matter what comes of it, it will still *always* be "Bill's hangar."

So here's what I take from Bill and all this: Airports and hangars are darn fine places to hang out, and it's darn-right okay to hang out there just as darn-much as you want. It's a "right fine" place to be, do, solve government's problems and, yeah, even go flying into the blue where others have gone before us and where they meet us again in spirit. So just keep doing it. It's good people, good feelings, and you're a part of a mighty fine legacy. And Bill would want you to take up the slack. There's fun to be had, and he would say, "Have all you can."

And what's to become of that skanky old carpet in Bill's hangar? Don't know. Maybe it'll show up in the Smithsonian someday. If it does, don't worry about stepping on it and getting it dirty. As Bill would say, "That's the way it's supposed to be."

29

DREAMS

Okay, fair warning, stick with me on this one. We're going to veer off the path a bit. I'm thinking it might be fun. Maybe revealing. But mostly fun.

When you first scanned the title of this column, you probably thought it was about day-dreaming about wonderful airplane careers or building your quintessential dream plane or flying to some exotic, fun destination. Nope, that's not it. I'm talking about the kind of airplane dreams pilots have while they're sleeping. Whoa! Now that's opening a private door into sometimes a strange abyss, isn't it? Hang on!

And don't tell me you haven't had some funky airplane dreams! You have.

Ya know, I've read a lot of aviation articles in my time but never one about aviation dreams pilots have while sleeping. There's probably a good reason for that. Often, after my bride reads my first draft of a column she'll say, "You're kinda unafraid, aren't you?" Probably so. It also helps that I'm not very bright. So.....with apologies to Freud....let's look into that place that is the pilot's mind at night.

I had a dream that I was in a big hangar with a DC-3. (I'm type-rated in the DC-3 so I'm not surprised my nighttime mind put me where it had.) Then the dream gets a little wacky. I climb into the airplane and walk up to the cockpit. There is a black button on the instrument panel, circled by a silver ring. I push the black button. The landing gear retracts. The airplane settles onto the hangar floor. And I'm thinking, "Somebody's not gonna like this." Then I climb out of the airplane, which now has a cover on it. I pull the cover off and the airplane shrinks. (You're still with me, right? It's a *dream.*) So now I'm thinking I can prop the airplane back up and get the gear down. And I do: I prop it up with some wood then reach in the side window and push the black button again and the gear comes down. But the airplane is still about half its original size and I'm thinking, "They're still not gonna be very happy about this." And that's all I remember about that dream. Whew! What the heck was that all about??!!?? Actually, don't answer that; I probably don't want to know. And *don't* write and tell me you found a shrunken DC-3 in an abandoned hangar in Keokuk.

Okay, it's time for me to get myself off the 'weird-dream-hook.' The idea for this column actually came from a reader/friend in Texas who mentioned in passing (big mistake!) a dream he'd had the night before. He dreamed that his airline had called him back to work. (He had been 'age-sixty retired' a couple years before.) Only thing was, they'd only let him fly between two city pairs: DFW-ORD and ORD-DFW. That's it. Back and forth. But he went back anyway. Except that when he went back to work he couldn't find his mailbox or his flight bag. Look though he might, they were nowhere to be found. And then he woke up.

I've had those airline dreams, too. I was parked at the gate after a flight and the First Officer was reading me the engine shutdown checklist. He had called for a particular switch and I *could not find it!* I looked left, right, up and down. Very embarrassing. He read the name of the switch again. Still, I had no clue. He was looking at me like, 'What the heck is wrong with you??!!??' The dream ended with me looking up at the overhead panel, my right arm raised but not finding the correct switch.

(I know what's going to happen: Some of my airline buddy/former co-pilots are going to write and say, "Lauran, no. That was no dream. That's just the way you were most of the time.")

Another friend from New York told me of a dream he had where he was flying a Tiger Moth that his friend Dick had sold long ago. No brakes and with a tail skid. No matter, there he was, flying Dick's airplane. Not sure how. Not sure why. Just flying along. And then he added, "Dreams are made of stuff like that. Logic be danged." Exactly.

Okay, this is for real, but it was pure happenstance. I turned on the computer and my homepage had an article about dreams. It gave a word and then suggested what it meant if you dreamed about it. For example, take the word "air." It said if the air was clear and sunny, success lies ahead; if it was cloudy, foggy or misty, then you're not in a clear frame of mind. Take from that what you will. Then there was the word "button." It said buttons refer to the need to find ways to keep certain things together. Fine, but they should have added, "Does not apply to DC-3's." And, of course, there was the word "airplane." If you dream about airplanes you are dreaming about 1) escaping from the mundane exigencies of the lower world, 2) freedom and 3) the search for a higher consciousness. All well and good, I suppose........except that 'higher consciousness' doesn't apply to any pilots I know.

Sometimes your buddies end up in your dreams. I was pre-flighting a helicopter. I know nothing of helicopters so I guess that's why my formation buddy, Nel, was in the dream. He flew helicopters in the US Army. The fueler kept asking me how much fuel I wanted. I had no idea, so I asked. One guy said six-thousand pounds and another told me twenty-thousand pounds. Big help, so I still don't know. But then, while pre-flighting, I found the tail-rotor shaft bent nearly ninety degrees. Something's not right about that! And then it dawned on me, 'Why am I pre-flighting something I don't know how to fly?' Where was Nel in all this? He was flicking me the same guff he flicks me in conscious life. *Some* things don't change.

Oh, and then….and then!….I dreamed about a list of pilot sayings. There were eighteen of them and I just know they were all grand, pertinent, to the point, witty and true. And they were all in capital letters. I so wanted to read them. Except….all the letters were scrambled. Scrambled like dreams are.

Okay, that's it. I'm scaring myself. I'm going to my hangar. A couple hours with my airplane and in conversation with the local 'Hangar Rats' and my feet will be right back square on the ground.

Sleep well.

30

AN HOUR TO REMEMBER

It looked to be a great day for flying. There was an overcast layer about three-thousand feet above the surface. The clouds were stratus, soft and smooth looking. The surface temperature was 55F and the winds were calm, the kind of day that just makes you itch all over to fly.

I was ready. I had my commercial, instrument and multi-engine ratings and 427 hours total time. I was current and eager. The year was 1968.

I had scheduled the Cessna Cardinal-- N29402 --from Abilene Aero, the FBO at Abilene Municipal Airport, Abilene, Texas. The Cardinal was almost new, part of Cessna's 'drive into the sky' marketing experiment. It was sleek and low slung, didn't have any wing struts but had wide entry doors. You simply stepped in and, like Cessna said, drove into the sky. The scuttlebutt around the FBO was that it was a little underpowered with four people on board. That didn't matter today because there would only be two of us.

The mission was for me to fly west to Howard County Airport, Big Spring, Texas, pick up my girlfriend and fly east back over Abilene enroute to Addison Airport, Addison, Texas. There we were to meet my girlfriend's sister and brother-in-law and spend the weekend with them. Was that a cool plan, or what??? I thought so.

I arrived at the Abilene airport early, wanted to take my time and savor the plan. I filed IFR. Didn't need to, just wanted to. I did it right there on a phone in the lobby where everybody could hear me: young, punk kid filing IFR. Was I cool, or what??? I thought so.

I walked across the ramp to the shiny green and white Cardinal. My charts and flight plan were all rubber-banded together. I placed my little package of surprise cargo in the glove box. I was careful with it; it had cost me $246.17. The pre-flight was fun because the airplane was new, the weather was good and the anticipation was high.

The flight to Big Spring was uneventful, even soothing. I taxied up to the FBO/terminal at the Howard County Airport and there she was, sitting in her 1963 Mercury Comet in the parking lot. She was proud of that car: it had fins, a four-on-the-floor and bucket seats. The right hand bucket seat would often fall over backwards if she popped the clutch. Her car payment was $35.97 a month, which she paid at the bank every due date, and her Daddy fixed her car whenever it broke. Life was good.

I shut the Cardinal down and walked over to the gate in the three feet high chain link fence. She got out of her car, grabbed her bag and walked toward me. She was shining in a ray of sunlight. Big smile, short skirt and long legs. Damn, she was pretty! I was putty.

After a short hug and a howdy we walked to the airplane. I opened the door for her. I noticed the glove box door had come open. My cargo! It was still there so I reached in and slammed the glove box door shut. She climbed in and fastened her seat belt. I walked around to the other side of the airplane, got in, and managed to touch shoulders with her while putting on my seat belt. That was distracting. What's up with that?!!? Cool pilot becomes all flustered and distracted! So I say to myself, 'Get your cool back, Mr. Pilot Man.' Starting the engine helped me get back in my pilot groove.

After taxi and takeoff I was back on mission profile. Plus, we were in the stratus. Nothing like gray in the windshield to get a new instrument pilot to concentrate. I taught the young beauty with the short skirt sitting on my right to listen for and copy down our frequency changes. She caught on right away. She was pretty *and* smart. I did my best to keep up my pilot façade so she wouldn't know what a goober I was.

The clouds gave way to clear skies about ten miles west of Abilene, on our route to Addison. My passenger liked being able to look outside and see things. I pointed out some landmarks, of which there aren't many in West Texas. I showed her Dyess AFB, where I was stationed in the Air Force at the time, and Abilene Municipal Airport. Over the Abilene VOR at 9000' the to/from indicator switched to a solid 'from.' I sort of wanted to talk about the intricacies of VOR navigation to display my technical prowess. But that wasn't on my mission profile. My mission profile called for something else, something I was now getting cotton-mouth-nervous about. I looked over at my passenger. She was looking outside, to her right. Her hair shone pretty in the light and her hands rested lightly on her lap.

I thought it would come out cooler than it sounded but it came out almost blurted, "Will you marry me?" The pretty head didn't immediately turn. Then it turned slowly. Then her eyes looked at me with....what??? Surprise???? Doubt??? Shock???? Wonder??? What??!!!??? How can fifteen seconds seem like forever? Then her words came, "Only if it's forever."

That little exchange resulted in a 300' altitude loss (no Mode C in those days) and a full scale deflection of the VOR needle. Oh yeah, the airplane thing......

I then reached over and opened the glove box and took out my cargo. I opened the small box, lifted the ring out, grabbed her left hand and slipped the ring on her finger. I only lost 200' this time. I was getting good at this.

Fort Worth Center called with a frequency change. It was the first I'd heard from them in a while. Or so I thought. They testily said they'd been trying to call me. Huh? I asked my new fiancé what the new frequency was that Center just gave us. She didn't hear it either. Fine pair we were hurdling through the sky.

Onward to Addison, mind and emotions going about a thousand miles an hour. Bachelorhood gone. Airport in sight. Tower gave us a straight-in. Long final. Low. Dragging it in. Sorry excuse for a pilot. Engaged!!! Getting married!!! Over the runway, nose up, still carrying a lot of power, more nose up. That all-moveable stabilizer really grabs the air. I chop the power and the airplane deems me a complete idiot and the left wheel prangs down on the runway followed by the right wheel followed by the left wheel again followed by the nose wheel then airborne again where the entire sequence repeats itself with only a little less severity. It was an impressive display of ineptness brought on by a total lack of concentration. In complete innocence, the pretty girl sitting next to me asked, "What happened?"

All I could come up with was, "Rough runway."

Okay, fast forward twenty-four years to 1990, 8727 flight hours and five type ratings later. We're in a Stearman this time, PT-13D, N8528N. Same girlfriend/wife, one-thousand feet AGL on a warm autumn day over the Willamette Valley in Oregon. I had to yell it over the intercom this time, what with a 300 horsepower Lycoming rumbling up front and a ninety mile-per-hour wind blowing in our faces, "Will you marry me?"

"What?"

"Will…you….marry…me?"

"Only…if….it's….forever."

The landing was better this time. It must have been because she left me a note on my desk at home, 'You stud. Loved it. Love you, K.' That's a lot better than, "What happened?" Besides, wives catch on to bogus excuses real quick. In fact, I think "rough runway" was the first and last one she ever bought-off on.

Now fast forward to 2005. With an anticipated completion date for our RV-8 of autumn 2005, guess when my next proposal is going to be? She has stood by me during my 'construction journey' all the way. And I need a good landing because, in aviation, I figure two-out-of-three is good enough. I'll keep you posted.

By the way, thirty-seven years later, she's still pretty and I'm still a goober.

31

DESTINATIONS

Flying is many things, all of which serve to make it the magical attraction that it is. It is mechanics, the joy of flight and destinations. Today, let's talk about destinations. There are many out there; there are many that are no longer there. The latter fact was recently brought home to my bride and me.

On our first wedding anniversary, I was a young US Air Force pilot stationed in Texas. During my off-duty time I was working towards my CFI rating, so I had access to a civilian airplane, the ubiquitous Cessna 150. So, what better way to celebrate our anniversary than to fly to some nifty destination? We had heard that the Lowake Inn (pr. Lo-wake-ee) in Lowake, Texas was *the* place to go. Okay, done deal. I started drawing lines on a sectional chart to Lowake.

In the flat country of Central Texas, there is not much to navigate on. You just sort of go from one town to another until you arrive at your destination. (For the younger set: we didn't have GPS in 'the olden days.') So that's what we did, until arriving over a small town at the end of our computed ETA. The town had a few houses and a couple larger buildings of some genre. And it had a wide, rectangular spot in the middle of a cornfield. The airport. We landed there, kicking up red dirt throughout the landing roll. We shut down the engine. Silence. Silence all around. Country silence. I looked over at my bride and said, "We're here!" She looked back at me with a "we are????" look. Romantically, she had worn the same outfit that she wore when we left on our honeymoon: a green and white dress with matching jacket and white shoes. A tall sign in the distance said "Lowake Inn." We had a corn field to walk through. But we were young so we went with the flow. We slogged through the corn and across a road to the Lowake Inn. Romantic that I am, I wiped the red dirt off her white shoes before we entered.

We stepped into the restaurant. One lean cowboy was leaning over the jukebox and Willie Nelson was serenading the patrons. It wasn't quiet but it got quiet as the other cowboys at the bar stopped talking and turned around to look at us. They didn't say anything but they didn't have to because it was obvious what they were thinking, 'Y'all ain't from around here.' The waitress waved towards some empty tables and said, "Sit wherever ya like." We didn't need reservations.

The menu was meat and potatoes and potatoes and meat. Mostly *big* steak and steak fries. Fine by me. The waitress was friendly and we managed to work it into the conversation that it was our first wedding anniversary. That got us free dessert and some tipping of hats and words from the cowboys, "Congratulations." Texas friendly.

I could go on but you get the picture. It wasn't exactly what we expected; it was better. It was better because it was friendly and real. You can manufacture "fancy" but you can't manufacture genuine hospitality. The Lowake Inn is a destination that we've never forgotten.

So, in August 2008, on our fortieth (!) anniversary, I wanted to re-create the journey of thirty-nine years ago. Not to fly from Oregon, where we now live, to Texas, but to fly to a 'down home' and fun restaurant destination. Out of curiosity, however, I searched "Lowake, Texas" on my computer and found this: "Lowake, Texas, Northwestern Concho County, Rural roads 1929 and 381, 9 miles NW of Point Rock, population 40 (estimated)." And under that, the very first picture caption said, "Very famous original Lowake Inn – it had a runway for fly-in customers." The picture was of a brown, closed, boarded-up, lonely looking building, but still with a sign out front that said "Lowake Inn." Time marches on. Another destination gone.

Undeterred, thirty-nine years later, my bride and I climbed into our RV-8, "Ohh Kay!!" and flew north towards Mt. Hood. There are lots of mountains to navigate toward in Oregon. My sectional was folded and tucked in my canopy side pocket: ready. But I didn't need it. Head towards Mt. Hood from Salem and you fly right over where we were going: Mulino, Oregon (4S9). We entered on a forty-five for a left downwind to runway 32. Paved runway this time, with some other airplanes on the ramp. Quite civilized. Still very quiet, however, after we landed and shut down. And we got to walk across another field, this one mowed, to "The Airport Café," nestled next to a two lane highway. No white shoes this time, though we talked about them. As well as the green and white dress with the matching jacket. This time it was athletic shoes and blue jeans. Comfort. And it was to breakfast. But no cowboys. Loggers and construction workers instead. Good company and another friendly waitress. And we talked of many things, of jobs, kids, grandkids, life, of destinations gone and new destinations. All in this funky, friendly, little café with a counter, booths and tables. Very real. Very comfortable. And I told my bride I loved her.

Mission completed. Another flight, another destination, another memory. A very good day.

All of which serves to remind us of other destinations. Some you can return to; some you cannot. You're thinking of some right now, aren't you? I once returned to the first airport I soloed from, Reid-Hillview Airport (KRHV), San Jose, California. It's still there, but so much busier now. That changes the charm it held when it was still out in the country. But I'm glad it's still there, because it's been a battle of survival with the city that has grown up around it.

And I've been back to the airport in the farm country where I grew up, Scott Valley Airport (A30), Ft. Jones, California. It was the airport I used to walk around, alone, before I was a pilot, but dreaming of becoming one. I'd walk to the middle of the runway and stand there, looking both directions...wondering and thinking. I wandered into every open hangar and lingered with the airplanes. The airport is little changed, still offering access and dreams. Very nice.

My former Air Force pilot training base is closed now, and has been for some time. Lots of tumbleweeds around the base buildings. It is still open, however, for civilian use, as a general aviation airport, McMahon-Wrinkle (KBPG), Big Spring, Texas. Many years later, I once returned in a military OV-1. As I flared over the numbers of runway 17L, for an instant I was a Second Lieutenant flying a supersonic jet once again. It was one of those eerie and fun feelings all at the same time. You can't go back in time, but you can recapture moments. And it feels good to do so.

But there is one place I have not returned to: the airport where I had my very first airplane ride, Siskiyou County (KSIY), Montague, California. My Dad bought two round-trip tickets on a DC-3-- I don't remember the name of the airline --from Montague to Medford, Oregon and back. My first flight! I remember the excitement, the noise, the rattle, the roar, the bounces.....and the magic. I became, that day, who I am today. The airport is still there, expanded years ago by the military, but still quiet and rural. I will return-- I *need* to return --to descend through the air that first took me aloft and flare over the numbers on runway 35. Why? It's a "pilot thing."

You know what I'm saying. We're pilots. Destinations call us. Go there. 'Tis good for the aviation soul.

32

LESSONS

It was a dark and stormy day. Well, at least right over the airport it was. Where we were, in the holding pattern, it wasn't too bad. We were in the clouds and it was a little bumpy, but nothing particularly out of the ordinary. Each time we made a circle in the hold, we got a glimpse on the radar of the weather in front of us over the airport. Big green splotches there. (We didn't have colored radar in those days.) Not a thunderstorm, just wetter than a wet dog. I was a new Captain. And I was hell-bent on getting the job done.

In my airline career I started pretty much at the low end of the scale, co-pilot on a Piper Navajo for $600.00 a month. Flew co-pilot for six months, then upgraded to Captain. I liked the Navajo: solid, honest and, within its imitations, quite capable. But then my airline moved into 'the big iron:' the Swearingen Metroliner. Nineteen seats, Garrett TPE-331 engines that made as much noise as thrust (but were very reliable), no autopilot, and with flight controls as heavy as a Mack truck without power steering. But, hey, it was a flying job. And I was the Captain in a holding pattern with nineteen people who paid money to get where they wanted to go.

The airport was a non-towered coastal airport in the Pacific Northwest. It was one of those places that could be three-hundred feet overcast with one-half mile visibility in heavy rain with the wind gusting thirty knots *across* the runway. Which, exactly, is what the weather was. And I was the relatively new Captain hell-bent on getting the job done. Did I already say that?

We were cleared for the approach. Okay, here we go! How bad can it be? On the transition radial from the holding pattern to the ILS localizer, not too bad. But.......getting progressively worse. And darker. Real dark. In the daytime. I turned the instrument lights to full bright. And it was getting bumpier, too. A lot bumpier. At one point my Jeppesen manual, which I had set on the floor between the pilot's seats, came off the floor and flew back and lodged itself between my seat and the bulkhead. That bumpy. The control yoke was built large. Now I knew why: you needed the size for leverage against the heavy controls. We were now basically stop-to-stop on the controls, and still bobbing around like a cork on the high seas. 'Wow! This is fun,' flashed through my mind. As did, 'Or stupid.' The localizer needle was just now beginning to come alive. At least I thought it was. Between my eyeballs bouncing in their sockets and the instrument panel bouncing around, it was more like looking at a kaleidoscope than an airplane instrument panel.

And then the rain hit, like being in a high-powered car wash at two-thousand feet. I turned on the windshield wipers and got a rapid slap-slap-slap-slap. Which resulted in a smear-smear-smear-smear on the windscreen. But 'smear' was the least of my worries right now. The engines? They were running like the thoroughbreds they are. The noise they make was suddenly a *very good* noise. Love those Garrett's!

I finally got the airplane onto what was a reasonable facsimile of a final approach course and glide slope. I probably looked like a wallpaper hanger trying to hang three sheets at the same time, both hands and both feet being very busy. The co-pilot? Fairly new to the airline, he just seemed to be looking out the window, not focusing on much of anything. Can you blame him? He was flying with an idiot.

While thrashing my way down the final approach course I realized it was taking about thirty degrees of left correction from runway heading to keep the localizer centered. 'Oh, yeah, the crosswind,' my overworked (and, some might say, underdeveloped) mind finally remembered. Five hundred feet to minimums. I took another glance out the front window: more smear-smear-smear. Back to the bouncing needles. The gear? Oh yeah, we already did that, just didn't feel it with all the bumps and gyrations going on. Three-green on the panel, though. Three hundred feet to minimums. Needles getting very sensitive now. Just what I need with all the turbulence. I continued doing battle with the needles. One hundred feet to minimums. Co-pilot says, "Runway, one o'clock." I looked straight ahead. Nothing. I looked at one o'clock. The runway. Except it didn't look like a runway. It looked like a very large rectangular puddle that had runway edge lights along the sides. I couldn't even see the centerline paint for all the water covering it. Which is why what happened next happened: almost full left aileron into the wind, nearly full right rudder to keep the nose straight, elevator to keep the nose up…..a little more….and….and…..and…..we touched down like a feather on new fallen snow. Blind luck….literally…with the smear-smear and all. But I'll take it.

We sloshed and splashed our way to the gate. Passenger service agents came, holding broken umbrellas into the wind, and opened the passenger door. The passengers filed off-- mostly silent -- but one sweet-little-old-lady-type walked into the cockpit. I turned in my seat and she bent and kissed me right above my right eye. She then backed away, stood straight, looked me in the eye and said, "Thank you!" She was tickled to be on the ground. I didn't tell her that I was, too.

We were scheduled for a fifteen minute turn-around. We were ten minutes late arriving. We now had five minutes to unload, fuel, load and leave. My mind spoke to me again, 'Not gonna happen. Relax.' As I was walking around the airplane doing the post-flight, a ray of sunshine broke through, almost spiritual-like. Off to the north was a very large, very dark cloud. I knew it well; we were not friends.

As I climbed back into the cockpit, the co-pilot was looking out the window at the dark cloud to the north, too. Then he spoke, "Wonder what it woulda been like had we waited in the hold a few more minutes before starting the approach?" I looked at him while nodding my head, not speaking but saying, 'You're right.'

We departed in clear skies, fifteen minutes late….diverting around one particularly large, ominous dark cloud to the north.

They say "all's-well-that-ends-well." I suppose that's true…as long as learning takes place. My airline that day, Air Oregon, was purchased by Horizon Air which was purchased by Alaska Airlines. Twenty-six years later I turned sixty years old and was put out to pasture. But, in those twenty-six years, I can honestly say that I never hurried another approach just to stay on time. Lesson learned. One of many lessons, it turns out. But the lesson that day taught me that you never stop learning. And that's probably the most important lesson of all.

33

FOOD FOR THOUGHT

If airplanes could talk, the stories they could tell that their pilots haven't.

Bad weather may be an excuse for a lot of things, but it should not be an excuse for abysmal performance.

An excellent landing at the wrong airport is an excellent landing wasted.

Haste is the leading cause of oversight.

Complacency is an insidious killer.

Flying a full-motion simulator is a lot like standing on a football.

The keys to success in an aviation career are hard work, proper procedures, trim and good radio terminology.

The more complicated a procedure, the more likely it will be done wrong.

Don't make a gear check on final. Make three.

The first requirement for a good landing is a good approach.

A decision to hold your bladder will be met by a headwind.

An overshot final is a dangerous final.

The most important limitations you need to know are your own.

Good basics early serve to make a good pilot later.

When the throttle goes forward the mind should be clear.

The more clearly it is communicated, the better it will be done.

Repeated practice is better than a one time performance.

You know you're getting old when airplanes you used to fly are sitting up on sticks at airport entrances.

If you don't know where you are you should at least know where you were.

The tops of bumpy clouds are bumpy.

If you are bored flying, your standards are too low.

If you are holding short wondering if you have too much ice on your airplane, you have too much ice on your airplane.

The best ice prevention device in the airplane is you.

Impromptu air shows for friends or relatives often result in death.

"Pilot error" is bureaucracy's way of getting everybody else off the hook.

"Get-home-itis" is a human emotion that often results in poor judgment.

Operations manuals should be more readable than voluminous.

Subtle differences buried in the text of complicated procedures are a trap for pilot error.

If you buzz people or things all you are really doing is putting your stupidity on display.

A peek in the gas tank is worth a thousand fuel gauges.

Don't land long on a short runway.

Land after you've been cleared to land, not before.

Know where the ground is at all times.

The best landings are made at the lowest possible speed.

In aviation, worse than poor planning is indecision.

Remember: a forecast is a guess.

The FAR's are written by lawyers, for lawyers.

In the twenty-six years I spent at the airline, the "proper" crew calls on an ILS probably changed seven times. It's still an ILS.

Definition of poor planning: well above gear speed, well inside the outer marker and it's three-hundred overcast.

An instructor without patience is not an instructor.

Training just to 'fill a square' is not training at all. It is square filling.

An honest mistake is not a sin. A mistake uncorrected, however, is.

An airplane graveyard is a silent monument to adventures past.

Landing gear are very strong to a point. Try not to find that point.

Aviation experts are oftentimes not.

A pilot's idea of a gourmet meal is a new snack machine.

Arrogance is often a cover for incompetence.

The simpler the airplane, the more pure the joy.

Get in the habit of centering the ball without looking to see if it is.

The media understands aviation like a hippopotamus understands flight.

A seat belt flapping outside a closed door is a good indicator of poor attention to detail.

On taxi, horsepower is seldom a match for a tie down chain left tied.

Impress your wife by not trying to impress her.

The trouble with these huge new manuals is that by the time I get to page seven-hundred, I've forgotten what was on page one.

The chances of a procedure being done incorrectly increase exponentially with the complexity of the procedure and the infrequency of its occurrence.

Airplane neglect should be a crime.

Better to slow down than let yourself be pushed by events.

A forced landing is a wing and a prayer.

If you don't know your CG, your airplane does. I recommend you be the first to know.

Pay attention in a crosswind, if you get my drift.

Fuel remaining is something you should have after you land.

If you hear, "Ultralight 234, radar contact," somebody's lying.

Being late ain't great, but it's better than making a mistake in haste.

Attila the Hun would be a lousy flight instructor.

A tailwind serves to make a short field shorter.

To keep a pilot from monopolizing the conversation, tie his hands behind his back.

If the regulations get any more voluminous or confusing we won't be able to fly without busting *something*.

Proper procedures are an antidote for accidents.

I've seen people who can't fly the simulator but can fly the airplane, but I haven't seen anyone who can fly the simulator but can't fly the airplane.

Deviations are for thunderstorms, not for procedures.

There is great satisfaction in a difficult job well done.

Here's what you say after you've passed a check ride: "Great ride. No questions. Thanks a lot. Can I go home now?"

The best way to do your job is to do your job.

When five different pilots come up with five different adjusted gross weights for a contaminated runway takeoff it is not the fault of the pilots. It is the fault of the manual.

Airplanes are not created equal.

Thunderstorms do not discriminate.

Freedom of speech is not guaranteed in aviation: say what you have to say on the radio then get off of it.

The slower the touchdown, the shorter the roll.

The bigger the plane, the bigger the salary.

The harder you study, the better you fly.

Flying is freedom, except you're not free to be stupid.

If you don't already have it, religion is something you get about the time you blunder into a thunderstorm at night.

Two things you don't want to be at the same time: confused and in the clouds

The more we regulate aviation, the less of it we'll have.

Fear of the unknown is natural, so the more you know the less you'll have to fear.

Make your corrections many and small.

Don't worry about mistakes. That's what flying is: correcting mistakes.

Take the time to thank your ground crews and mechanics.

The further ahead you are the better off you are.

If it doesn't feel right, it probably isn't.

The approach is more important than the touchdown.

Confidence is good; arrogance is not.

Hours and airplanes don't make you fly good: flying good makes you fly good.

If you're trying to salvage an approach, don't. Start over.

Don't do something because you think you can; do it because you *know* you can.

Know what you're going to do before you get there.

Do everything with a reason.

Always have an option.

When you're hoping the weather will get better the best place to be is on the ground.

Be aware of what's going on around you.

The thing about a professional is that he's *always* a professional.

If airplanes could talk, rental airplanes would have to most to say.

When the rain that was beating on your windshield gets quiet it has become ice.

Don't be afraid of your airplane, just respect it.

Do not wear a necktie in a J-3. It is socially incorrect.

Writing about flying is not easy. You feel more than you can describe.

There would be a lot less animosity if passengers would get it through their heads: on-time means same day.

Small town airports are generally inhabited by colorful characters.

Passengers are trusting. Make it well founded.

The less you rely on luck the longer you'll have it to use.

Tall trees at the departure end of a short runway are ugly.

Don't fly up a canyon under an overcast that obscures the mountain tops. Your options narrow at the same rate the canyon does.

A locked brake on landing is an excellent diuretic.

Fatigue is the enemy of good judgment.

A propeller is a loaded gun.

Don't do anything that someone might later be able to construe as being stupid, because they will.

Don't wear good clothes around old airplanes.

Most all aviation feats have been accomplished with great perseverance to a background chorus of naysayers.

A flight in the morning calm can serve to make the whole rest of your day go better.

Flying is the human spirit unchained.

34

IN THE COMPANY OF AIRMEN

In 1966 I drove my Volkswagen Beetle down California and across the plains of West Texas to Webb AFB, Big Spring, Texas to attend US Air Force pilot training. I was twenty-two years old, with a flat stomach and could see a fly speck at five-hundred yards. And I was about to begin, in earnest, my childhood dream of becoming a pilot. As I neared Big Spring I could jets on the horizon, circling, taking off, landing, climbing, banking. Literally, the sight made me tingle all over. I pulled over alongside the road, got out and stood, taking it all in. All I could think was, 'Save some for me because here I come.' My sign-in date wasn't until the next day.

Sixty-three of us signed in; forty seven of us graduated. For the next fifty-three weeks we did nothing but eat, sleep, and drink aviation. There were tests and pressures, but I don't remember that bothering us much. Mostly I remember the flying: we flew nearly every day, up, down, around, over, straight up, straight down, spun around, rolled and looped and flew lots of instruments and formation, all in airplanes that know few limits. After the first time I went supersonic I wrote in my logbook, "My life's complete." Was that year special? Yeah, you could say that. When we graduated we were awarded silver wings to pin on our uniform. Do I still have them? Yup, they're sitting on the corner of my desk as I write this.

After graduation, we scattered to different airplane assignments, to different locations, to different lives. Some made careers in the military; some served their time and became airline pilots; some served their time, returned to civilian life and never flew again. But, no matter, because none of us ever forgot that one year in our lives when we became pilots and banded together as brothers in arms.

Now it is 2009, forty-three year later, and my bride of forty-one years and I drove down the very same road that I drove on in 1966. Only this time, as we neared Big Spring, there were no jets in the air, my "abs" are a little more rounded, and I'm wearing eyeglasses. The base closed in 1977 and time changes things and anatomy. But my mind still remembers that year in great and joyous detail. (Secretly, I'd sign in and do it all over again for free.) And that's why we returned.

The townspeople-- not the government, the *townspeople* --were holding a reunion for all who ever served at Webb AFB. And all who served at Webb AFB remember the townspeople: some of the nicest and friendliest people you'll ever meet. When I walked into a store in Big Spring in 1966, they'd say, "Hi! How y'all doin'?" When I walked into a store in Big Spring in 2009, they said, "Hi! How y'all doin'?"

The government closed the base but the townspeople kept one hangar, preserved it, and found and put on display one of every type airplane that ever served at Webb: an AT-11 (from when it was a bombardier school during WWII), a T-28, T-33, T-37 and T-38, along with a lot of other artifacts. Today it's called the Hangar 25 Air Museum. And, on this one weekend, many who served returned to remember and honor their time at Webb AFB.

And the memories flowed and eyes misted looking across the expansive but now barren flight line ramp. Friendships were renewed and new ones were made. And the stories flowed, too. My class mate and T-37 table mate reminisced, "I remember the time I wasn't feeling too well and our instructor, Lt. Hassen, insisted on doing spins that day in the T-37. I think he did it on purpose. We must have done fifteen of them." Military flight training is known for its "no slack" ways. Sink or swim. That's how the game was played. I loved spins in the T-37. If you popped the stick forward just right to break the stall, your head would hit the top of the canopy. The more scratches you had on the top of your helmet, the cooler you were. Dave made it, flew aerial tankers, rescue helicopters in Vietnam, and commanded a missile squadron. He now owns a successful infrared imaging business in Southern California. And that was a recurring theme among my classmates: most everyone who finished pilot training has done well in life. They learned the concept of work and reward at an early age and it served them well.

And there were poignant moments, too. At one of our dinners a wife stood and said, "My husband was a pilot, got shot down and was listed as missing in action. He never came home. But people like you never stopped being my best friends. That's why I'm here." And my bride and I stood in Hangar 25 and struck up a conversation with Richard, an African-American man from New York. He said, "I was stationed here in the 50's. Drove the tram that took the pilots to and from their airplanes. I was nineteen. One day my Lieutenant took me downtown and said, 'Let's go in here and eat.' I said, 'I can't go in there. They won't serve me.' But we went in and they did." Stories like that make the hair on the back of my neck stand up. I said, "I'm sorry you even had to consider something like that. But I thank you for your service and I'm proud to know you."

Then Julius Jayroe spoke at another of our dinners. He, too, had served at Webb AFB. In 1967, he was shot down in an F-4 over North Vietnam. He spent six years-- *six years* --as a POW. Think about that for a minute. How do you get six years of your life back? You don't. And, yeah, he was tortured: they put his hands in shackles behind his back and hung him by his arms. Many times. But here's what he had to say about that, "We made the best out of a very bad situation. We had to. I won't say it made me a better person. That'd be a stretch. But it gave me a keen insight into the human mind. The mind, left alone, is almost limitless. I mean, that's all we had left to defend ourselves. One of my fellow POW's remembered the names of one hundred twenty-five other POW's. We had to lean on and learn from each and band together to survive." Julius related the story of another POW who commented, "I wasn't very religious when I came in here, but I am now." When asked what religion he embraced, he said, "All of them." Julius is home now and remains proud of his service and of those who serve. He said he is no hero; he was doing his duty. I beg to differ with the "no hero" part.

At that same dinner, the two-hundred in attendance stood and sang the National Anthem. Sang it loud. And they all knew the words. And you *felt* it. And all of this story because we were once stationed and trained in Big Spring, Texas at a base called Webb. Some think the "brothers in arms" thing is a little corny. We don't.

35

STEVE

I want to tell you about Steve, but it's not going to be easy. Why? Because Steve doesn't talk about Steve. He's a legend around the home airport, but he's a shy legend. And a humble legend. Oh, he'll talk to you........it's just that he doesn't talk about himself. Steve is, however, a worthy topic. I've pieced together, from here and there, bits and pieces of information about him. It's the bits and pieces that make up this story. When you finish it, you'll know what I mean when I say Steve is special.

I'd heard about Steve but first met him on the day he received the Wright Brother's Master Pilot Certificate. It's awarded by the FAA upon recommendation *and* fifty years of flying without violation or accident. In Steve's case, it's actually been sixty-five years, but who's counting and that's beside the point. The point is that he's been flying well for a long time and darn well deserved the award. Of course, true to form, when Steve walked into the room where the ceremony was held, and a bunch of his buddies had gathered, he said, "I'm not sure all this fuss is necessary."

Before the ceremony commenced, somebody in the back of the room hollered, "I guess getting shot down doesn't constitute an accident?"

The FAA official in attendance answered, "That's correct. It does not."

You see, Steve was shot down in WWII while flying a P-38. He was captured and spent three and a half months as a POW. Somebody else piped up with, "Were the Germans mean to you?"

Steve answered, "They were Austrians." And that's all Steve had to say about that.

I'm going to let you in on one of Steve's P-38 missions. But I didn't hear it from Steve. I got it from a written post-mission debriefing report: "F-5 (P-38 photo aircraft) escort mission Foggia to Munich area, Jan 1945. 4 P-38s, 25,000'. 2 ME-262 jets descending through high thin overcast almost collided with P-38s. No prior warning either flight. P-38s immediately switched to internal fuel, started descending to separate from high clouds and attain more agility, and formed Lufberry circle. Tight circle with only 5 aircraft including unarmed F-5 but 1 or 2 had rotating visual contact with 262s at all times. 262s circled flight at about 2 miles for a few minutes, then departed. (Note: Big disappointment. If they engaged they were toast – in our humble opinion.) Completed photo mission and returned to base with all 10 150gal drop tanks still in place. (Note: I think the squadron supply officer awarded each pilot a cigar for this feat.)"

When asked about the story, Steve said, "Somebody-- wasn't me --insisted that we scared off the 262s with our tactics. But the intelligence officer wasn't buying it. It was pretty obvious that the 262 pilots either were looking for bigger fish, probably B-24s, or were low on fuel or ammo from a prior engagement." Steve being Steve again.

Steve later flew P-51's and then the F-86 in Korea. On his first combat mission in the F-86 in Korea, he shot down a Mig. It's in the record. Steve doesn't go around telling about it. He just doesn't see the need. He's from the school of "just doing my job." I've always been of the opinion that pilots who don't have to talk about their flying, don't, and those who do, do. Steve falls into the former category.

When the FAA representative handed Steve the award, Steve shook his hand, said thanks and looked down at the floor. He was then asked to tell a story. Horrors! Steve doesn't tell stories. So what did he do? He said, "I wish I could tell you I had fifteen or twenty thousand hours, but I don't. Or even ten thousand hours. And I don't have a type rating." So here's this guy who has been shot down, captured, flown P-38's, P-51's, T-33's and F-86's and he's talking about what he *hasn't* done. Typical Steve. Oh, and did I mention that he's eighty-seven years old and still owns and flies a Cessna T-210? And that the CFI who gave him his last BFR wrote a letter of recommendation (one of many he received) for the award praising not only his dedication to aviation but his professionalism and precision as well? I mention it because Steve doesn't.

It was probably the gentleman within him that led him to acquiesce and tell one story to the crowd. His eyes squinted slightly as he paused and gazed toward the ceiling. He said, "I learned to fly in 1940 on the other side of this very airport (McNary Field, Salem, Oregon). It was the Civilian Pilot Program for the military. My instructor's name was Vern. We were in a J-3 and I was sitting in the back. Vern could see that I didn't have my feet on the rudder pedals. I saw him looking at my feet but he didn't say anything. When we got on the ground he came right up to my face and said, 'How do you expect to fly the airplane if you don't have your bleeping feet on the bleeping rudder pedals?'" Steve said he thought Vern was flying the airplane, but thought better of saying so. He simply took his verbal lashing like a man and from that day forward, he never took for granted who was flying the airplane.

Someone in the gathered crowd muttered under his breath, "That's the longest story I've ever heard him tell."

Steve's eyes squinted again as he began with, "There was that night in a thunderstorm in a T-33." But then he paused, looked back down at the floor and said, "But that's a story for another time." Steve was back in character.

Steve is from a generation of doers, not talkers. I know a bunch of politicians who could take lessons from him. And there aren't a lot of "Steve's" left, so when you meet one, honor him/her. They'll reply with, "Aw, shucks," but deep down they'll appreciate your appreciation.

There's a flip side to this story. Steve honors honor. He'll tell you that all the "Steve's" of the world are not just WWII vets. Many are veterans of more recent battles and they, too, are like Steve: they do much and talk little. Honor them, too. I can assure you that Steve does.

I'll close with this tidbit: Steve was born on July 12th. It is the only day, since the National Weather Service began recording the weather, that rain has never fallen in Salem, Oregon. It fits. Steve is, indeed, a ray of sunshine.

36

FLYING BUDDY

Once in a while, along the aviation pathway of life, you get a flying buddy. It's generally someone who thinks about flying the way you do. You bond as friends and you bond as like-minded aviators. Neil is my flying buddy.

We met while serving in the National Guard. I was already in and flying when Neil came aboard. First thing we noticed: Neil was older. Like late forties older. What's up with that? But he met all the requirements for entry, including the unwritten "likeability factor," so the powers-that-be signed him up. In a unit that flies a single pilot airplane, like we did, Neil still had to earn the most coveted thing: respect. But that only comes from your squadron mates…..later.

Neil had flown the F-86D in the US Air Force, for the 54th Fighter Interceptor Squadron. A long time ago. In the meanwhile, Neil had been busy making a living and raising a family. That took his time and resources. And it took him further and further away from flying. But the demands of living never took the flying *out* of him, only *away* from him. Some give up on ever flying again; Neil never did. Even on his lowest day, the flying ember stayed lit.

He became successful in business. That's not surprising; he's a 'stand-up guy.' He found himself with time and money. That allowed him to check-out in some civilian airplanes. That was good….but not quite good enough. For once you have tasted the sky with a stick and ejection seat and canopy, it is *there* that you long to return.

Neil had driven by our National Guard unit at the airport many times and had noticed…..and coveted……our airplanes parked on the ramp. The OV-1 is a little awkward looking, has a lot of angles. But it's also a little sinister. Seductive, even. And it has but one set of flight controls. (The right seat has the surveillance equipment, but no flight controls.) At first, the doubts crept in (don't they always!) and he thought, 'Naw, no way they'll let me in this late in the game.' Later, time slipping by, he told himself, 'Dangit, there's only one way to find out. I gotta talk to them. I gotta try.' So he did and, long story short, he was accepted.

Neil went to the aircraft qualification school. He shook off the rust with sheer determination. When he returned to the unit, he quickly became known as "the born-again aviator." He would fly anytime, anywhere. He was a scheduler's dream; he never said no to a flight. He was, to put it mildly, glad to be back in the air. It was obvious to all that his part-time National Guard job took precedence over his full-time civilian job. But he made it all work quite nicely.

All of the above is how we came to be flying buddies. Before Neil joined us, I was the one known as "the time hog." I wasn't out of military flying as long as Neil had been, but I felt the same way about it that he did. I mean, good grief, if the military hands you a single pilot airplane full of gas, you fly it! It's a gift…never to be taken for granted. Soon we became known as "Time Hog One" and "Time Hog Two."

As National Guard pilots, we met once a month to fly. But flying once a month was not enough to maintain proficiency. So they gave us what they called AFTP's (Additional Flight Training Periods) to use for additional monthly flying. No matter how many they gave us, Neil and I always wanted more. Single pilot units develop a special camaraderie. We generally celebrated that at "Happy Hour." But on the weekends, if there was after-hours flying, Neil and I always volunteered for it. We liked to party as much as the next guy, but we liked to fly more.

As a Guard unit, we attended several "Red Flag" military exercises at Nellis AFB, Nevada. There, all services come together to hone their skills. Our mission was tactical reconnaissance/surveillance. There were a lot of "happy snaps" during the daytime missions but somehow, probably because Neil and I never objected, we were generally known as "the midnight dogs." Neil would fly the 'high cover' radar detection missions and I'd fly the lower level infrared missions. Much goes on at night in military operations so we were generally pretty busy with targets. Being roommates, we'd usually get back to our hooch, after the night's flying, around 4:00 AM. There we'd discuss the missions……and life. Neil would pull out a bottle of wine and sip it and munch on dry toast. You know those nifty military flight suits with all the pockets? Truth be known, in the lower left leg pocket, Neil carried dry toast. No matter. All anyone really cared about was that he flew the mission and he *always* did that. And, yes, by now he had the respect of everyone in the squadron.

Once I was assigned to fly an aircraft to a base and leave it. Neil was the pilot assigned to pick me up. On the way home, I fell asleep in the right seat. Neil always told me, "That was the best compliment you could have paid me."

It's hard for me to believe that everything I've told you thus far happened some twenty years ago. Time flies.

Recently, I was telling another "Neil story." I was telling of the time when we were somewhere, at some military exercise, and we were assigned, temporarily, six to a room. Well, "Ranger Dan," as we called him, could snore loud enough to raise a roof. I remember it being around 3:00 AM and I opened one eye and saw Neil silhouetted in the doorway, dragging his sleeping bag with one hand and carrying his pillow under the other arm. As he slipped out of sight, I heard him say, "I can't take it any more." He went outside and found a truck to sleep in. It was Neil's caregiver, Deb, that I was telling the story to.

You see, not long ago, Neil and his wife Betty, her brother and his wife, were visiting Yosemite National Park. Neil said, "I have a headache." He lay down and the headache went from bad to real bad. And then to a stroke. He was airlifted to a hospital in San Francisco and it was nip-and-tuck. The emerging star became Betty. She fought tooth-and-nail for him. For those of you unfamiliar, stroke recovery is a long road. Long and arduous. Betty has been by his side *every* inch of the way. And still is.

Neil can sit in a chair now and can stand, for short periods, with the aid of a walker. He can mostly speak, albeit in a whisper. Part of his face can smile. But his eyes-- his eyes! I can look into them and I know he's still there. He just can't get all the way out.

During a recent visit, Betty got his old flight suit and jacket and laid them on his lap. He looked at them for a long time. Then he touched and rubbed the aircraft patch on his jacket for an equally long time. I knelt beside his chair and said, "Ya know, buddy, it's about time you get off your butt and get down to the flight line. You can't expect us to carry your dad-gum load forever." He looked at me with those eyes; he *knew* what I was saying. Then, with some effort, he gave a thumbs-up.

And if he could, he would. And it would be midnight. And his toast would be in his pocket. And I'd be pre-flighting the aircraft right next to his. At the end of the runway, I'd watch his red, rotating beacon takeoff into the black of the night. And I'd takeoff right after him. I'd follow him anywhere. He's my flying buddy.

Our unit mission being reconnaissance, we used the call-sign "scan." Each pilot had his own, individual number. I was "Scan 14" and Neil was "Scan 19." To this day, we still call each other "One Four" and "One Nine."

Godspeed on your recovery, One Nine. We've lots more targets to get.

37

THE SPIRIT

You know it's going to be a good day when you are in the run-up area, sitting in your airplane, idling, and the sun is flickering through the propeller, sending morning rays of joy into your cockpit. The airplane feels good around you and the anticipation of camaraderie and the pancakes at your destination fill your soul. Yeah, this is a good day.

I've had a lot of 'aviation good feelings' this summer. I call them "the EAA kind." Yet the EAA is not a rule making body; we don't bow down to it or conform to it, per se. Nothing about it is mandatory. It is simply a spirit, a spirit recognized a long time ago by a guy named Paul Poberezny. He envisioned the need for like minds to band together and share. Little did he know how well he "envisioned."

The spirit now abounds all across this great land (and, indeed, the world). We all approach it a little differently, with different opinions and airplanes, but the one constant is the love of flight. That constant-- that togetherness --is what has allowed us to grow and survive. United we stand; divided we fall. 'Tis a law of nature…and politics. Never forget that.

Okay, I'll get off my soapbox. Let's jump from the genesis to the everyday joy that is the spirit of the EAA.

We're back in the run-up area. We're flying to a chapter pancake breakfast-- EAA Chapter 902, Mulino, Oregon to be exact. It's a beautiful morning. There are going to be lots of airplanes and lots of pancakes and a country western band and old cars and old tractors. (Pilots gravitate to all manner of machinery.) And there's going to be a formation fly-by by a group of RV pilots.

The day before the breakfast I learned the time and location of the rendezvous point for the final practice session of the RV formation group. (Loose lips sink ships, Nel.) I orbited above, undetected, and watched them join up. Then I trailed them high and to the rear. (*Never* would I join-up without first being involved in the pre-formation briefing.) I followed them as they made several passes over the airport, well above pattern altitude, and as they changed formations on the outside downwind. Think about it: a bunch of experimental airplanes and their pilots doing something that challenges them because they enjoy the challenge. Watching them go round and round, I was struck by their discipline (probably the most important part of legitimate formation) and...their spirit.   This   small   group   of   seven-- builder/pilots sharing and spreading the joy of flight. A microcosm of Paul's vision. A slice of Americana. It felt good just to witness it: it was "the spirit" on display above palette Earth.

And now, the next day, I was in the run-up area at my airport readying to fly to the pancake breakfast where they would be performing, only this time I'd be watching them from the ground. As would a lot of other people. But this breakfast wasn't just about a formation group. It was about a lot of things, machinery, flying, visiting and, yeah, pancakes.

I was cleared for takeoff. Power up, the airplane rolls and the tail comes up and the airplane gets light on its wheels and leaves the Earth behind. Flight! Always magical; forever magical. Nothing now but you, your airplane and the morning calm. There's just something about it: when the air is smooth and the weather is clear it makes you feel good. And, somehow, everything you look at is good. Fields, farms, river, towns. You see the ryegrass and the fescue in the fields ready for harvest and you imagine the harvest to be a good one; you see farm houses and barns and you envision good people in them, drinking their morning coffee, discussing and getting ready for the day; you see the river and picture families swimming, fishing, picnicking, floating and boating; you see towns and you imagine people waking slowly, talking softly, and smiling gently, readying themselves for a relaxing day. Is all this really happening? I don't know. But from my vantage point -- aloft on a new morning in an airplane I built with my own hands --I imagine it so and just let it go at that. It's 'the flying feeling' to the tenth power.

I tuned in 123.05 for the Mulino Airport. It was busy. Lots of people flying to breakfast today. But, guess what, all were professional, patient and courteous. Necessary radio calls only, no jabber, no jerks and all standard traffic patterns. Good people; good pilots. I was proud to be among them.

I landed and turned off the runway and there they were, the fixtures, the standards, the icons of the EAA spirit: the volunteers. People in red vests with red paddles directing me-- and a lot of others --to parking. Every one of them smiling. Now you tell me, how can you not feel good at a time like this? It's welcoming, camaraderie, fellowship, and aviation all rolled into one friendly little ball: a chapter pancake breakfast. Chapter 902 did itself proud right off the bat!

Parked, I was unbuckling from my airplane when a man and woman walked by and the woman took a picture of the nose art on my airplane. I hollered, "That's my bride when she was eighteen and we were dating. We've been married for forty-one years." I don't know why I said all that, but I did. She said, "That's so cool." It was a brief moment of friendship with like minded strangers. I love stuff like that.

I wandered the grounds at little Mulino Airport. Airplanes galore: RV's, Swifts, a Zodiac, Sport Cub, Steve Johansen's RV-3B, AgCat, Stearman, Cessna's, Piper's, Waco, TavelAire, Stinsons, Kitfoxes, '55, '56, and '57 Ford Thunderbirds (a nice man explained to me how to tell a '56 tail light from a '55 tail light), and a 1931 Case tractor. I was like a hog in slop. Paul P. started it; EAA Chapter 902, today, was the poster child for his vision.

The pancakes were not slop. They were perfect, as fly-in pancakes always are, and cooked by members of the Oregon Pilot's Association, Mulino Chapter. (United we stand, remember?) Polite, happy, industrious, hard working people gathering for a meal on a beautiful day, surrounded by airplanes. You feel it, too, don't you?

(As a side note: they served 775 (!) breakfasts that morning. How's that for a couple small aviation groups banding together for one day at a small airport!!)

While we were in line at the breakfast, Gary Dunfee pulled his RV-6A through the line, such that the line had to split. I approached him with, "Sir! Sir! We're trying to run a breakfast here!" He just smiled and said, "Hey, Lauran! How are ya?" He was on his way to fly some Young Eagles. He's passionate about that. If he's not the leader in Young Eagles flown in Oregon, he's at least toward the very top of the list. He's quite a guy!

And then eight RV's flew over in formation. Very nice!

As I was standing in line, I was talking to Nel. I was telling him that Steve Johansen, a hangar neighbor, won an award at Arlington for his RV-3B. Nel pops off with, "When you gonna enter your plane for an award? Like for most pinholes in the paint." That's my buddy Nel. But, hey, somebody has to be his friend; no body else likes him.

A little more about Nel. If I were to try and sell him on a street corner for a nickel, I wouldn't get two cents. And even if I did, it'd be two cents more than he's worth. But he flew down to my airport a while back and we did what we do: flew formation. We brief, start together, taxi in formation, wing takeoff (those are just *so* much fun), fly fingertip, cross-unders, close trail, extended trail, re-joins-- all that stuff --with brief radio calls, hand signals and airplane signals (wing rocks, rudder wags, etc.). He leads and then I lead. Why do we do it? Because we love it. We built these little RV-8 quasi-fighters, we're both ex-military and enjoy the fun and challenge of it all. It's like an expression of freedom. It's the EAA spirit, pure and simple.

Then we land, taxi in and shutdown in formation, de-brief and then I buy lunch. I always buy lunch. (Well, not really. I just want to hear him bellow after he reads that.)

Okay, I know, perhaps I've waxed a little too poetic here. But here's the deal: these last few weeks of summer have been poetic. Good weather. Good flyin'. Good people. And I'm very thankful for all of that. And I know you know exactly what I'm saying.

There's just one more thing to say: "Thanks, Paul."

38

FIRST FLIGHT: RESTORATION

This isn't about the first flight, as in the impending one in my under-construction RV-8, or about my first solo, but about *a* first flight. First flights have a way of searing themselves into a pilot's permanent memory, and this is about my first flight in a Stearman that a partner and I restored.

A few years back my partner and I found and bought a partially restored Stearman. All we had to do to it was install the engine and finish the myriad details involved in preparing a restored airplane for flight. Homebuilders and restorers often say that a project is 90 percent finished with 90 percent of the work to go. 'Tis true. A lot of the little things take time, many are unexpected, and, of course, there's the circuitous bureaucratic journey to obtain the required paperwork. But restorers/homebuilders are not faint of heart. They persevere. And we did just that. It took two years, but we finally got the airplane ready to fly.

Then came the day to actually fly the dang thing—which it hadn't done in seven years—with a newly installed zero-time engine on its nose and me, with no Stearman time, to fly it. We decided that I'd fly it because I had more total time, was more current, and had time in various taildraggers.

I'm not real bright, but I'm bright enough to know that it's folly to jump into an airplane you've never flown—and try to fly it. That's an invitation for trouble. Trouble often comes when you're not looking for it, let alone when you're asking for it.

Previously I'd run the engine many times, and I'd taxied the Stearman a lot, down the runway, tail high. Under these conditions it felt pretty much like an airplane, but the forward visibility was lousy when the tail was on the ground. Always in the back of my mind was the Stearman's reputation, so I called my friend who is current with lots of Stearman time and asked him to give me some Stearman dual. "Sure," he said, casually adding, "It's a pussycat on grass and a wildcat on pavement." Hmmm...It turned out he was right, especially with an extenuating circumstance.

It was a nice day, calm, very blue sky, with a little apprehension thrown in, but still fairly comfortable. I'd strapped in, started it, and taxied several times. At idle, a round engine is soothing music to any pilot's soul.

Our plan was to leave our small, narrow strip and fly the short distance to a larger non-towered airport with more runways. We'd do a little air work en route, you know, to get the feel of the thing. Ailerons, elevator, sounds, slow flight, stalls, steep turns, pressures, visibilities, stuff like that.

I never worried about the airplane; good grief, the Stearman has been around for ages, training (and humbling) pilots since World War II. It's built like a box and strong as an ox. I just wanted to explore and experience its personality for myself.

We'd do some landings at the big airport, full stops—mandatory to experience the full regime of the Stearman on the ground—to get comfortable with the airplane. Then we'd take her home to the drums and flourishes of a successful test flight. A modest beginning (except for the drums and flourishes), but airplane beginnings should be modest. (My former-Marine buddy, Ed Kolano, is a great believer in modest test flight beginnings, but after reading this he's going to chew up and spit out my airplane judgment this day.)

So there we were at the end of the runway, run-up complete, ready to go. No going back now. You work months, years, for this day, and then suddenly, it seems, it's here. The moment. The now. It's humbling. It's sobering. But it's time.

You line up, peering around the sides of the long snout that is a Stearman in a three-point attitude. Nothing much on your mind except getting this thing off the ground gracefully. I mean, what else could matter at this point. Power up. Be ready on the rudders. A little tap here and a little tap there. The nose begins to wiggle one way, and you tap the rudder the other way. Not very effective at first. It takes big taps. But, as the speed builds and the sound increases, it takes increasingly smaller taps.

The tail comes up. You're ready for that; you've done it before. You gain an almost respectable amount of forward visibility. The thing is still going pretty darn straight. You don't feel it, but you're sure your friend in the front seat is but a millisecond from the controls. Then the thing gets light on the mains. And dang! You're airborne. Just a little at first, the runway falling away slightly, then, seemingly, a lot, with countryside visible everywhere. A quick glance to the side, and you see bystanders standing beside the runway. Your family is among them.

Yow! Airborne! You can see straight up and straight down, unrestricted. You've never flown an airplane like this before. And the wind! In your face, down the back of your neck, and up your pant legs at 90 mph. And the lack of noise...the engine is so far forward that you can't hear it so much as you feel it. This is a horse of a different color! But what an ambience. For a minute you're a 19-year-old kid off the farm in Iowa down at Randolph Field in Texas, learning to fly this thing for the Army Air Forces. You're feeling history here. More people should feel history the way EAAers do; it adds a wonderful perspective to life.

Something else is happening, too. The first five minutes of flight have completely washed away all the frustrations, bloody knuckles, and doubts of the past two years of restoration work. It was all worth it. Totally worth it. You'd been flying the same airliner for the past eight years, probably 2,500 flights in that time, and while you enjoy your work, not a one of those flights was even close to what you're experiencing on this first flight in a Stearman. This is not work; this is life.

Air working the Stearman toward the big airport, the airplane is solid, even heavy on the ailerons, but very honest and straightforward—at least in the air. Your partner up front passes a strip of paper to you—the Stearman has neither radio nor interphone yet—that has a figure with MPH on it. You're slightly puzzled because your airspeed indicator is in knots, a fact you scribble on the paper and pass back forward. Hmmm. Miles per hour in front and knots in back. How in the heck did we miss that? Your partner sends another note. You see "60K" before the wind snatches the paper from your hand.

The big airport comes into view. You gaze intently but see no one in the area. Good. You don't relish embarrassing yourself before witnesses. The wind is almost directly down the widest, longest runway. You fly over the airport and gently slide into a left downwind. All's well. The airplane is purring, the air is smooth, all's stable.

Turning base now, powering back, you begin slowing. Airspeed's right where you want it. The long nose is an excellent pitch reference. On final now. Visibility okay so far. Pavement under you now. You raise the nose. Visibility over the nose is gone. Runway is so wide it's difficult to pick out equidistant references. Where's the ground? How the heck should you know? You've never landed this thing before.

So this is what absolute inexperience feels like. Where are the wheels? Forward, yes, but how long is the gear? It must be getting close. From previous taildraggers you know that slow is good—as long as you're close to the ground when the thing plops on the runway. Clunk! There? Stick back, the tailwheel hits, and the mains come off the ground again, just a bit. So there's a bit of a crow hop. But full aft stick, and no airspeed to speak of, takes care of that. Then a slight swerve to the left. Tap right rudder. Harder! The swerve becomes smaller, manageable S-turns. You're on the ground, rolling out, under control (sorta)! You're not quite sure how it all happened, but it did.

A horse of a different color prances through your mind again. The other taildraggers you've flown aren't the same: A Citabria is a pussycat; a Cessna 140 is springy, but its performance is docile; when dropped a Champ just spreads its gear, recovers, and rolls straight; and with a DC-3 you must be on speed, but the forward visibility is good and the gear wide, so it tracks straight.

The Stearman. First impression: with long narrow gear, lousy forward visibility, and a bunch of the weight forward with the big round engine and small tailwheel way back there, well, it all adds up to an easy swapping of ends. Bottom line: It requires your full attention on landing.

But you made it, so you taxi back for another circuit. The airport is deserted, but a car has pulled over to the side of the road that parallels the runway, apparently to watch. Stearmans are cool.

Takeoff is normal, downwind normal, final normal, flare normal—still feeling for exactly where the runway is, however—then touchdown, a slight hop, then something! A clunk! The tail rises, the left wings come up, the nose points toward the runway, and you correct left—overcorrect left. The left wing comes down, the nose comes back up, tail goes down, and the airplane comes off the ground again. You're now slow and crooked to the runway. You correct right, and the airplane lands again, pointed about 20 degrees off center-line and headed for the weeds. You stab left rudder, and the airplane changes direction enough to stay on the pavement, thankfully low on airspeed and energy now. You roll to a stop. You think the airplane is insulted.

In a situation like this you don't continue to taxi. You sit. Then you slowly exhale all the pent up air sucked in and retained. Then you taxi— slowly—off the runway, park, and shut down the engine. Then you sit some more. Then the goggles and helmet come off, and your friend (ex-friend?) turns around, and you see that his eyes are as big as yours as he says, "What in the golly-gosh-dang-it was that?"

"Dunno."

You climb out. The car is still beside the road, entertained to the max. With a story to tell, it leaves. You walk around the airplane. It appears intact. No scrapes. What about the clunk? You push the airplane back a little, then forward. It makes a clunk and lurches a little toward the right. The right brake! It's catching or something. Crud! Now what? Deserted airport (I know, Ed, bad plan, but I hadn't planned on staying there), no tools, cell phones not yet invented, and people expecting us home in 30 minutes. We don't show, and they start worrying.

Looking all around the brakes as best we can, we can't see much. Lines okay. Connections okay. No leaks. Pedals okay. No stray pieces lying about. You rub your chin and ponder. No way home. No way to call. You push the airplane around some more. No clunks. You decide to start and taxi it and then try the brakes some. No clunks. All the while you're getting closer to the end of the runway.

Then you're at the end of the runway. Engine running. No clunks. Never clunked before. Just this one time. Must get this thing home. Friends and family waiting, wondering. Get-home-itis? Yup. You've read about it a lot. Usually not good. You linger a moment longer with thoughts toward flying. Your partner turns his head. You point toward home and raise your eyebrows. Your partner gives a thumbs up. And, just like that, you go. Power up, tail up, airborne. And instantly you wonder, "Did we do the right thing?" There's only one thing worse than one pilot making a bad decision—two pilots making a bad decision. But hope springs eternal.

Flying home all thoughts are about landing. Don't pay much attention to the guy on the combine below, looking up. He doesn't know you're pensive, sitting on the edge of the seat, not leaning back. Narrow runway to come, plenty long, however, with friends and family waiting, watching. Alternating thoughts: Why am I up here? What a dunce! It'll work out. Wheel land. Tail down slowly. Don't use the dang brakes.

And that's what you do, wheel land. You stick it on the runway, forward visibility okay. You let it roll. Tail down slowly. Directional control is actually easier to maintain on a narrow runway, better landmarks. And you let it roll all the way to the end of the runway, energy dissipating. Then you brake—ever so gently—to slow enough to turn off the runway. No clunks. You taxi in to smiles and waves. Do you sense relief on your wife's face? If she only knew. You sense it on yours.

"How'd it go?"

"What a sweetheart. Little brake problem, though."

"Sure looks purty in the air."

"Thanks."

The Stearman maintenance guru steps up, "Brake problem? Did it grab?"

"Yeah, you might say that. Actually, yeah, it did grab."

"Yeah, those stock brakes will do that sometimes. I'll look at it." You savor your family and friends while the brake gets checked. "Hey, that screw was a little loose, which allowed this widget to contact the framitz. Probably wouldn't notice it at a slow speed, but at a higher speed it might be an issue if jostled just right. It's fixed now. That screw probably hasn't been touched in 30 years."

Such is life, huh? You just never know. But you can't live in fear. Every decision is not correct. And you live and learn. Sometimes you're just lucky. I couldn't tell this story to just anyone. They wouldn't understand. But I can tell it in Sport Aviation because EAAers do understand. They've been there.

39

FIRST FLIGHT: HOMEBUILT

Incredible. That's the word that comes to mind when I think of the first flight in my RV-8. But it was more than that. A lot more. It was exciting, rewarding, wonderful and magnificent all at the same time. It was all of the above.

Those of you who have already completed first flights know exactly what I'm saying. Those of you who are building have it to look forward to.

Last month I talked about the first engine start. That was exciting but even more exciting was that the ball started rolling pretty fast after that. All the parts were now becoming an airplane that was going be to ready to fly.......soon.

First was the airworthiness inspection. Actually, I felt pretty good about that. I had put my heart and soul into building the airplane and, while I knew it wasn't perfect, I'd had three Technical Counselor visits-- essential, in my book --and had tried very hard to do the right things. And if I didn't know how to do the right thing, I asked. The cosmetics of the airplane are not that important to me but the mechanics of it are. I guess that's the farm boy in me. I also had attended Joe Gauthier's certification seminar at AirVenture last year and used his checklist, a very good one. And I used KitLogPro, which has all the required forms to be filled out, all neat-like, on your computer. Of course, I had all the pertinent FAR's and handouts, too. (The EAA now has a certification packet for sale but that came out after-the-fact for me.) I knew, especially after twenty-six years with an airline, that the paperwork is at least as important, or even more so, than the airplane. So when the inspector, David, walked into the hangar, I had every bit of paperwork laid out in order with every "i" dotted and every "t" crossed. He didn't say much about it at first but later he said, "You were well prepared." I liked hearing that because I had worked hard to be just that.

David walked around the airplane with flashlight and inspection mirror. The only thing he found was, "There's about a matchbook cover width between the mixture arm and the stop." (One twist back on the stop-nut, one twist forward on the turnbuckle and two twists back forward on the stop-nut fixed that.) It kinda hit me as he was walking around the airplane that the inspector is there to check general airworthiness and make sure the paperwork is in order but the actual responsibility for the airworthiness of this airplane was mine. All mine. And that's a responsibility I don't take lightly.

When David left I had an airworthiness certificate for N214KT. "Wow," I said to myself, "this thing is legal to fly!" The airplane and I just sat together in the hangar for awhile and looked at each other. Maybe you have to be a builder to understand what I just said but you builders know *exactly* what I'm saying.

The next day I journeyed to the Federal Lair (aka FAA) and got my Repairman's Certificate. As the inspector, Mike, was going through my builder's log another emotion hit me: I'm going to miss my project. There'll always be plenty to do on it but the 'creation stage' was over and that was a special time….and now it's already a memory.

Next? Call Mike Seager for RV-specific transition training. He's a busy guy, instructs nearly seven-hundred hours a year in RVs, so I couldn't get on the schedule with him for another week. At my hangar I'd look at the sky: blue. I'd look at the windsock: limp. I'd look at my airplane: legal. I've been flying forty years and have seven type ratings and have taildragger time in a Citabria, Cessna 140, Stearman, Champ, Pitts and DC-3. And then I'd say to myself, "Lauran, don't do it. It is not the professional thing to do." I settled the debate I was having with myself and waited the week. During that week, Karl, a reader, visited my hangar and said, "You have a quote in your 'If Airplanes Could Talk' book that says, 'He who checks himself out in an airplane runs the risk of having a fool for a flight instructor'". Exactly. Thanks, Karl.

On May 18th I drove to Scappoose (yes, Scappoose), Oregon and met and flew with Mike Seager. We flew an RV-7 for three hours (two flights) and did air work and pattern work. I felt good about the air work and needed the pattern work. The training was invaluable. In my book, if you haven't flown RV's before, it's dang near mandatory. Put your ego aside. Mike has more RV time than anyone on the planet.

He has both the demeanor and expertise to make you a safer RV pilot. I'm not slighting Mike's training by only discussing it briefly here because I'm going to devote my column to him next month. I feel that strongly about what he's doing. He's making a difference in this world…..one pilot at a time. He's also a Flight Advisor. Between Mike and my other Flight Advisor, Jack, in Cicero, New York, I was ready.

On May 19th the sun shone brightly at my hangar but the forecast was for rain in the afternoon. (I live in Oregon-- rain is a way of life.) I never wanted to set a date or invite a crowd to the first flight. I only wanted to do it when the airplane was ready and I was ready-- when it *felt* right. The only person that I really wanted there was my bride.

I opened the hangar door and there sat N214KT-- ready. Eager, even. I sat in the cockpit and reviewed what I had learned the day before and went over what I wanted to do on the first flight. I had it all memorized. I then pre-flighted the airplane, slowly and methodically. I know the airplane well but I wanted to establish a habit pattern, a good habit pattern. I pushed the airplane into the sunshine. It shone like a new penny, proud like. I called the tower on the phone and told them it was a first flight and discussed my plan of staying over the airport. They were both interested and accommodating. I then called my bride to tell her to come to the airport.

Enter "life."

My bride was at the hospital. Her Mom, 88, had fallen but everything was now under control. She said, "She's fine but I just don't think I can leave right now."

I said, "I can fly another time."

She asked, "Do you want to go now?"

I said, "I really kinda do." It was just feeling like "The Time." And it was supposed to rain for the next four days.

She said, "Then do it."

I said, "You sure? I can wait."

She said, "No. Go."

As an afterthought, since I changed insurance companies (my former insurance company does not insure first flights) to EAA's plan, I added, "The new insurance papers are on my desk."

My bride started to cry.

I asked, "You okay?"

She said, "Yes, just a lot going on right now. Call me right after you get on the ground."

I said, "I love you." And with that I strapped in and began my checklist. A lot going on, yes, but I'd learned a long time ago that when the seat belt goes on the mind must go clear. I was ready.

The airplane's engine started just as easily as it always has. The oil pressure came right up. Noise, vibration, good pressures and temperatures, it was time to taxi. At the end of the runway the run-up was as it had been before during engine runs, everything 'right on the money.' For some reason, as an afterthought, I ran the engine at full power for thirty seconds. Why? I guess my subconscious wanted a boost. It got it-- the engine ran loud and clear.

The tower said, "Cleared for takeoff." I barely heard them. Just previously I had been thinking of all the parts I had put together on the airplane. But when I pointed the nose down the runway all that went away. I was calm. In Mattituck I trusted.

Power up, tail up, tickle the rudders to keep the nose straight, check to see if the airspeed indicator works-- it does --light on the wheels now and next thing I know......we're FLYING! I climb straight ahead and then begin a left turn out of the pattern. I look out at the left wing and the ground and say loudly to myself, "This is incredible!" (There's that word again.) I leave the power up like they told me to do to 'seat the rings' in my new engine. I make gentle turns. I check temps and pressures. Then a little slow flight to a power off stall with full flaps. Airplane is as honest as the day is long. I fly along some more and then I call for a right downwind entry to runway 31. I fly the pattern like Mike taught me. No guessing. I already knew what to do and how to do it. And that, exactly, is the value of transition training.

On final now, runway flashing under me, gentle touch on the controls (transition training again) to a gentle touchdown to a slight swerve as I moved my feet from rudder pedals up to the brakes. Tower cleared me to cross the other runway and switch to ground and asked, "Everything go well?"

"Sweet as sugar," says I.

Power up to cross the runway, fumble with the radio to change frequencies, pull the power back, get left index finger tangled in the mixture control by the throttle and manage to shut the engine off, coast clear of the runway with the prop stopped and add, to ground, "Until I did that." Turned ignition key and my faithful SkyTec starter came immediately to the rescue and in no time engine and prop were doing what they're supposed to be doing when you taxi: be running. Tower said nothing and neither, later, did any of the gathered crowd of locals. And believe me, if they had seen it happen, they *would* have said something. Dodged a bullet there. Why am I now telling 170,000 people that I accidentally shut down the engine on the taxiway? Because I've never pretended to be perfect, just real.

I taxi in and shut down. I didn't want to get out of the cockpit. I wanted to savor the experience. A small crowd gathered. Steve handed me a bottle of Jack Daniels. I held it. He took a picture. He took the bottle back. I never saw the bottle again. It started to rain. I got out of N214KT, bonafide airplane, and pushed it back into the hangar. I called my bride. All is well.

I got home and my eighty-eight year old Mother-In-Law was there, in bed. I sat next to her and put my hand on her shoulder. In a weak but clear voice she invoked a WWII term with, "Way to go, flyboy." Day complete.

Vital statistics: seven years and 2500 hours of building. Weight: 1034 pounds. Engine: Mattituck TMX0-360. Prop: Sensenich 72FM (85). Instruments: whiskey compass and inclinometer. Avionics: ValCom VHF. Paint: Krylon rattle-can. (I used to make my living flying frough-frough airliners. I'm through with frough-frough.) Bottom line: 200 mph for right around forty-grand. That ain't too shabby.

What a wonderful construction journey it has been with my bride of thirty-eight years with me every step of the way. I thank her and I love her. I say again: Incredible!

40

SMALL AIRPORT AMERICA

co-written with my bride, Kay Lyn Paine

The plan for our journey to Oshkosh began seven years ago. It started as an idea. It then became a dream: build an airplane and fly it to AirVenture. I was still working at the airline at the time but the rude and wrong age-sixty rule was looming. After retirement, the building and flying process was to be the punctuation mark on my aviation career. And a wonderful punctuation mark it turned out to be: from the learning and satisfaction derived from the seven year building process, to my bride of thirty-eight years and I plunking down on runway 36L at Wittman Field in our homebuilt airplane on July 23, 2006. The journey was one of pure aviation joy. Quite frankly, it's difficult for me to imagine my life after retirement without the homebuilt. That's a strong statement, I know. But for me it was *that* fulfilling and *that* rewarding.

The 'putting pencil to sectional chart' part of the planning started as I was flying-off the forty hour requirement of the certification process. There I was, on the floor, on hands and knees, with sectional charts spread before me, with a 'mileage string' made from dental floss, thinking, 'This is exactly where I was forty years ago.' Perfect. My airplane is day VFR, by design. I wanted minimum technology and maximum joy. That's where I started forty years ago and, after military and airline careers, that's where the great circle of aviation life deposited me: on the floor with sectionals. And that's all just mighty fine with me.

It did occur to me during the planning process that I'd been spoiled the last few years. At the airline I had people who did all the planning stuff for me. They gave me a gate and a tail number and handed me a filed flight plan, weather, NOTAMs and a schedule. All I had to do was fly. Maintenance item? Call maintenance. Weather question? Call dispatch. Coffee? Ring the flight attendant. There were a couple times on our Oshkosh trip that I looked up and saw contrails and all I could think of was, "Slackers!" Now? VFR charts, dental floss and my Flight Guide.

The planning goal was to land at uncontrolled fields (that had fuel and motel listings). And we did that, with one exception I'll mention later. We planned two to three hour legs so as to stay within our physiologic comfort zone and to be able to land at a bunch of small airports. We wanted to 'sample' small airport America. And that turned out to yield some of the best parts of the trip. Small airport America is not flourishing but it is alive and full of good people.

The trip from Oregon to Wisconsin is roughly fifteen-hundred miles, across the Rockies and high plains. Many of you have flown to AirVenture so I hope our story mirrors yours and encourages others. Flying across America in a homebuilt is a wonderful adventure.

Trip planning, as is often the case, was intertwined with life events. I flew-off my forty hours and my first passenger, as it should be, was my bride. It was bumpy. I could see her hands gripping my seat back frame. So I climbed for smoother air. I saw her hands relax. We landed and pronounced ourselves ready. Two days later we 'married off' our youngest son in a beautiful wedding. Two days after that we climbed into a loaded N214KT, took off, turned out of traffic from Salem, Oregon and headed east. Clear skies. Smooth air. Familiar territory. Five minutes later my bride says, "There's a plane!" I looked up and, sure enough, there was the belly of a Citation. The *close* belly of a Citation. I looked left and he appeared to be on a long straight-in for Aurora State (UAO). Aurora State is a busy, uncontrolled field-- it is home to Van's Aircraft --and the Flight Guide says to fly the pattern. But that doesn't always happen. I tried to explain such to my bride and added, poorly, "There are risks." Needless to say, she became an *excellent* spotter after that. Breathing rate now back to normal, we were officially underway, VFR, no dispatchers, no autopilot, chart on legs, finger on chart. First scheduled stop: Ontario, Oregon.

Some say it was a leap of faith. Climb into a recently completed homebuilt airplane and fly across 2/3 of the United States, over plains and lava flows and jagged peaks. Just the two of us. Make that three.

The airplane soon took on a very personal identity. To take that leap, two things were constants in my mind. One was the integrity of the builder, and two was the confidence in the skills of my pilot. Not to mention that I like him a lot, have for a very long time…ever since we met at the Wagon Wheel Drive-In one summer night in 1967.

So, it was without trepidation that I climbed into that shiny silver and red RV-8 on a hazy Salem morning in July. I had one introductory flight, and a bumpy one at that. This was a new day and a new adventure. Shoving a couple of homemade airsick bags, a bottle of water and a notepad into a pouch by my right knee, I strapped in and gave a thumbs up. How romantic was this? A roll down the SLE runway and we slipped into the wild blue, headed straight for the Cascade Mountains.

The ride across Oregon was pleasant. It was smooth and the scenery was familiar. Letting down to Ontario Municipal (ONO) the bumps began. It figures; it was a hot day. There was one airplane departing the pattern and two crop dusters working west of the field. We plopped down on the runway and taxied to the gas pumps. They were near an old hangar that had wooden pallets and old airplane parts stacked about. And there were a bunch of former military airplanes parked here and there that were in various stages of restoration. We rolled the canopy back and were greeted with a blast of hot air. And silence. We crawled out of the airplane, teeming with the excitement of being underway to Oshkosh. More silence. And not a soul in sight. Our greeting was a sign on the self-serve pumps: " INSERT CARD HERE." Well…alrighty then. While fueling ($4.00) a crop duster taxied by. I waved. He nodded back. Another duster went by. I waved. He just looked at me. I figured he thought of us as runny-nose hobbyists. He had no idea how much I admire ag aviators. So much for basking in the glory of our journey to AirVenture.

We departed Ontario between crop duster passes. It was my first hot/high/heavy takeoff in our new airplane. It rolled a little further and the oil temp crept up to 220F in the climb. At cruise it settled back down to 185F. All in all, our airplane was answering its call to duty nicely. Enroute, east of Boise, Idaho the bumps began in earnest. We climbed. Still bumpy. And it kinda hit me: here I am, in this little airplane in this big world, with the most important person in my life right behind me, now getting bounced around the sky across the high plains of Idaho. I said, "Sorry for the bumps." She said, "I'm fine. Don't worry about me." It was the beginning of a bond, born of adventure, that grew ever stronger as the trip progressed. Next stop: Driggs, Idaho.

Romance aside, it is very sobering to see the belly of a shark (make that Citation) right over your head. Words were slow to form, like expressive slow motion. "Ummm, there's a plane...right up...there...is...that supposed...to happen?"

After that, I became perhaps the world's best airplane spotter...

With perfect skies and silky air, the string of volcanoes that make up the Cascade range were stunning. As we bounced into Ontaria, we were greeted only by the ghosts of old airplanes and a few crop dusters. Might have been a few rattlesnakes lurking in the shade, it had that feeling. Hot and dry, it reminded me of home, West Texas.

At Driggs (DIJ), the density altitude was 7200', it was hotter'n blazes and the wind was gusting *across* the runway. I opted for a wheel landing. Bounced it. In the bounce I decided, since the airplane was straight, to three-point it so I could stick it to the runway this time. But I only managed tail low. You tail dragger pilots know what that means: I hit with excess speed left over from the wheel landing. Bounced again. The third time-- fortunately --was the charm but with a lot of 'rudder walking' to keep it straight in the gusts. All my bride managed was, "Wow." Dang poor excuse for a pilot she was riding with that day. A rocky beginning but Driggs was nice. They have a spectacular new facility with the Grand Tetons in the background and a restaurant with a flying warbirds museum adjacent. Trevis fueled us ($4.50 less $.40 if you were flying to Oshkosh) and Rachel collected our tie-down fee ($5.00). We hitched a ride to the motel, tired but with leg #1 of our adventure notched.

That three hopper landing definitely brought me out of the clouds into Driggs. In the back seat of the RV-8, you can't really see the ground, and your depth perception is a little askew. I later learned to hunker down and not look out when landing.

The folks at Driggs were hospitable and the facility first class. Their Warbirds Café features WWII era nose art and a creative menu of freshly prepared meals. The setting is a picturesque valley, gateway to the Grand Tetons and the Rocky Mountain range. Farms and ranches, many with log homes, skirt the airport. If they hadn't offered a fuel discount for pilots on their way to OSH on the internet, we might never have discovered this great stopover.

The next morning I felt like a wet noodle. Was it the altitude? Life events fatigue-- fly-off, wedding, and packing all crammed together? (The bad landing?) Or all of the above? Not sure but since there were thunderstorms east of the Rockies, we took the day off. It was the right thing to do. That afternoon we walked to the Driggs airport and wandered about. We meandered south to where a MiG was parked. Mike Ward walked over and introduced himself. He knew of our plane, saw it on the ramp and put two-and-two together. He invited us into the hangar where the toolboxes (and his homebuilt) reside. Now I was in my comfort zone. Turns out Mike and crew were packing for Oshkosh, where they perform the "MiG Fury Fighters" show with an FJ-4 Fury (the only one flying) and a MiG 15 and MiG 17. The hangar visit got our AirVenture juices flowing again. Thanks, Mike.

The next day we were bright-eyed-and-bushy-tailed again. We left Driggs and turned toward the Tetons-- the *very large* Tetons. Upon recommendation of the locals, we wove our way through the Teton Pass. The Tetons were impressive, beautiful and forbidding all at once. It is times like these that you bond with your engine. And your oil pressure gauge. We dropped off the Tetons, or so it seemed, to the valley below, appropriately named Jackson Hole, Wyoming. From there, more mountain passes, down the hills and through the valleys to Riverton, past Casper, to Douglas, Wyoming for fuel.

The canopy in the -8 affords incredible visibility and it was a bit surreal to look out beyond those short stubby wings and see the craggy peaks of the Tetons below*! Crystal clear lakes and rich green meadows in the high Rockies unfolded beneath our wings. We were lighter than air, flying where eagles fly and in those lofty moments, I finally came to realize what drives people to fly. It frees your spirit, puts life into perspective, and soothes your soul.*

At Douglas (DGW) it was high, hot and gusty again. Wonderful! This time I stalled it, straight, twelve inches off the runway, in a three point attitude and it stuck....firmly. Which is as it should be…..thankfully. There were a couple of helicopters parked, part of a fire fighting operation, and a kid in the FBO who came out and fueled us ($4.00). After a PRP (Physiological Relief Pause), we were airborne again, this time to our next overnight stop, Gordon, Nebraska.

Whoa, back to reality as we plunked on down the runway at Douglas. Flying into small airports has its own charm. No fast food places, stop signs, traffic jams. What we found were friendly folks eager to talk with us and wish us Godspeed. The couple of Blackhawk medevac helicopters sitting on the ground were assisting in fighting the prairie fires twenty miles away. The National Guardsmen manning them were doing their civilian soldiering and we waved a thank you as we took off. The Dad of one of the crew chiefs was there to watch his son at work. He was a good 'ol boy and shared his flying history with us. The crews waved back, acknowledging our Vietnam Service ribbon proudly gracing our fuselage. Soldier to soldier.

Enroute, we finally found relatively smooth air at altitude and it was a welcome relief. Letting down for Gordon (GRN), it became hot and bumpy again but there was a crosswind runway and what looked to be new asphalt with new paint. We plunked down with only a slight skip and swerve and taxied towards some buildings/hangars. Yup, new asphalt. The parking spots weren't painted yet. We parked over some tie-down ropes. No people were about but we were greeted by three horses fenced nearby. They stared, with ears up and tails swishing. I'm a farm boy; that's plenty good enough greeting for me. We entered the building on the ramp. Nobody home. Outside, a white car of middle age vintage was parked. It had a hole in the roof. It turned out to be a former police car. The hole was where the red light had been. Inside there were radio wires hanging about, a holder for the microphone and no rear door locks. The front doors were unlocked and the keys were in the ignition. Deeming it the courtesy car, we started it and drove off. The shift lever moved but the shift indicator stayed in 'Park.' The radio played classical music. We couldn't turn it off or on or change the station. It just played classical.

Gordon, Nebraska will forever have a special place in my memory. Small town, big tractors, heartland of America. They take their patriotism, their families, and their football very seriously. By nightfall, I think *everyone in town knew who we were. We drove our 80's era Crown Vic right down to main street and went into the Stockmen's Drug. One of Gordon's finest police officers greeted us and we said, "We took your car". "Good," he replied. Then he told us to call the Rushville Sheriff's Office and ask for the on-duty Gordon officer when we needed airplane fuel. We asked the lady at the counter where to eat dinner. She said the restaurant at the Hacienda Motel, which is where we were staying ($37.50). It was frozen in the '70's. The nice lady at the drug store said "We go there every Friday night". Good enough for us.*

Knowing there would be a drive-in restaurant, we drove down a few more blocks and found the Covered Wagon Drive-In. I could eat there every day for thirty days and be happy. You actually drive through the covered wagon and stop at one of two windows. Saving our appetites for the Hacienda, we quenched our thirst with large sodas and found our way to the motel.

That evening we went to the Hacienda Restaurant. Grilled cheese sandwich: $2.00. Roast beef dinner: $6.50. The lady from the drug store and her husband walked in and the waitress handed her a beer. She saw us and said, "They know me here." Against the back wall was a long table where a group of people were seated. One gentleman sported red suspenders and had a red handkerchief hanging from his back pocket. He was 'go to town' dressed up.

A lady from the big table walked up to me and said "Do I know you? You look like somebody I should know..." Her name was Vicki. To tell you the truth, I think I could live in Gordon. I'd hang out with Vicki and the lady from the drug store and go to the Covered Wagon Drive-In now and then. I'd bomb around town in that old Crown Vic and people would wave and smile. It's that kind of town. Thanks Gordon, Nebraska.

The next morning we drove our former police car to the airport. The horses greeted us again. We called the Sheriff's Office for fuel. The on-duty officer came along with the off-duty officer, who had the key to the pump, and his son. Son's t-shirt said NEBRASKA FOOTBALL. Imagine that! Being in Nebraska, I kept my personal football allegiance to myself. Fuel was cash only ($4.10). Ten gallons topped us off. I gave the sheriff two twenty dollar bills. I didn't have a dollar bill and he didn't have change for a five. He said, "Aw, forget it." With that we bid our farewell and extended our thanks for a delightful visit. Next stop: Sheldon, Iowa.

I was learning a lot about flying in a very short time. Feeling like a seasoned flyer, we saddled up in the early morning light and left Gordon. The horses standing by the fence looked a little sad as we performed our preflight. The little town faded from sight, the big grain elevators standing tall in the distance.

Sheldon, Iowa airport sat right smack in the middle of cornfields loaded with ripening corn. Just what you would expect to find in Iowa. There was a rustling breeze through the corn, more like a whisper. Very quiet. Three old faded enameled lawn chairs were lined up by a hangar, red, yellow and blue. Empty now. I wandered inside and met Bob. Bob welcomed us and told me to sit. SIT. Sit down and I will climb in your lap and purr loudly and snuggle with you. So I did and he did and when we were done, he returned to his pillow tucked between the front window and the mandatory old sofa that every airport has. I put a quarter in the Frito machine and there it stayed, delivering no Fritos. I figure they pay for Bob's food this way. Glad to contribute.

Across Nebraska in the morning, it was smooth. Very nice. Crossing into Iowa, it was beautiful. Their agriculture was in full bloom; from above, the earth looked like a well manicured lawn. Nestled in the corn was Sheldon Regional (SHL). The wind favored runway 33. I saw no traffic and heard no traffic so landed on 33 and taxied to the end and up to the gas pump. Canopy back. Warm. Silence again. Wonderfully different from landing at Los Angeles International (LAX). There was corn to the left of us and an FBO-type building to the front. Not a soul about. I tried the door to the FBO and it opened. I heard, "Meow!" And out walked a cat. A friendly cat. He demanded attention and I obeyed. There was a wall phone with some numbers by it. I called one of the numbers. A nice lady answered and said, "I'll get somebody out there." A little later the phone rang and I knew the cat wasn't going to answer it so I did. Voice on the phone said, "Need gas?" Says I, "Yup." Says he, "Nobody there?" Says I, "Nope. Just me and the cat. What's his name?" Says he, "Bob. Tell ya what…." and he proceeded to tell me the secret location of the gas pump key. Then he added, "Get your gas. We'll knock some off for fueling yourself. Just put your name and address and how much you got on a piece of paper and slide it under the office door. We'll bill you later." I love this country! I came back from fueling ($4.00) and "Bob" was in my bride's lap. We bid our farewell to "Bob" and away we went again. Next stop: Prairie du Chein, Wisconsin.

The landscape beyond Iowa turned to perfect farms with silos and the richest green fields. We crossed rivers and floated through clouds in our little silver and red plane and the first raindrops of our trip dotted her canopy. Crossing the mighty Mississippi (I had to say 'mighty', it IS), brought thoughts of trade and industry, romance and literature, stories I had heard since childhood. My father-in-law had worked on a riverboat for a time in his youth. There it was below us, Old Man River.

This was to be our last stop before OSH. We would need to be close enough to have plenty of fuel and energy as we neared our final destination. Prairie du Chein turned out to be another great experience thanks to the hospitality of Richard Glenn. He greeted us with a smile and a welcome and after fueling the plane, offered us a ride to our motel. Richard is the chamber of commerce of the airport.

Onward to Prairie du Chein (PDC) we had to go over some clouds, around others and, close in, under others. Crossing the Mississippi River it was hot, humid and windy but the wind was down the runway for a change. We touched down and taxied to the gas pump. Yet another beautiful small airport. Richard, of Aviation Concessions, met and fueled us ($4.39). Richard said he came to Prairie du Chein eighteen years ago and never left. He has a Cherokee. He drove us to our motel in his car. He would not take a tip. We had prime rib and a nice chardonnay that evening. The next morning we got a motel van ride to the airport. Again, the driver would not take a tip. I wished the doom and gloom media would experience the America that we were experiencing. Next stop: Wittman Field, Oshkosh, Wisconsin!

I chronicled the flight from Prairie du Chein to Oshkosh in my October '06 "Plane Talk" column in *Sport Aviation*. We've been to AirVenture many times but this was our first time to *fly* there. Flying there, to the homebuilder's mecca, in our homebuilt was, for lack of better words, very, very special. It might as well have been 1953; the feeling was the same. As homebuilders, we were at the epicenter of the show; all else is wonderful but it's peripheral. We were one of 880 homebuilts registered. We got a patch and a mug. The patch is on my hangar bulletin board and the mug is on my office bookcase. Complain about the bigness of AirVenture all you want but I'm here to tell you that the 'homebuilding heart' is still there. We experienced it and it was meaningful and wonderful.

The flight from Prairie du Chein to Wittman Field was very quiet. We had read and re-read the NOTAM published just for arrival and departure into OSH during AirVenture. We were ready and rehearsed. But arriving that morning at the second holding pattern at Green Lake was something I could never have prepared for. We slipped into the gaggle of 150 to 200 planes circling like gnats over the water. My head nearly swiveled off from spotting planes. Seven to ten planes filled the front windshield at any one time. I didn't have time to be nervous, we had to stay very focused. The airport had closed due to a tragic accident that morning. "Ever see anything like this before?" I asked my pilot. "Nope, not in forty years of flying", he responded. Whew, I thought, this is hairy!

After an hour and half, we finally got clearance to land. It was a great moment to turn that little plane into her parking space and quiet her motor. She had carried us many miles. She deserved her rest and some proper adulation. As we walked away that afternoon, I looked back and quietly thanked the little plane for our safe deliverance. We had bonded.

The show went on and we sampled it. It was grand. We spent time at our airplane and met some very nice people. I even managed a nap (or two!) under the airplane. And, a new experience, we fretted when the weather channel spoke of thunderstorms. In fact, we were going to leave on Sunday, the last day of AirVenture, but delayed because of forecast sixty knot winds and possible damaging hail. Now *that* put a knot right in the middle of my stomach. But all we got was a good drenching. We watched the last performance of the show. As the smoke dissipated the show simply ended with.......... a whisper.

We left for home the next day and saw something we'd never seen before: AirVenture in repose. No buses. No volunteers. No entry gates. No people. It was like a ballroom the day after New Years Eve. Wittman Field had become......an airport. Kinda nice and kinda weird all at the same time. We loaded up, almost the lone airplane parked in the grass, and talked to Wittman ground control. Novel! I told him we were somewhere near warbird parking. He cleared me down taxiway P1 to runway 18. We then talked to the tower and he cleared us for takeoff. Looking down, AirVenture was packing up. Another year. Another show. Another great memory.

Turning out of traffic, homeward bound, the tachometer quit. Great! Five minutes later it came back. Our little airplane was not only dependable; it was magical. And, I'll tell you right now, that's the only mechanical thing that went wrong the whole trip. And that was only a temporary wrong. We love our little airplane! Next stop: Fairmont, Minnesota.

The Midwest was baking in 100F temperatures. Bumpy? Oh, yeah! We landed at Fairmont Municipal (FRM) for our fuel stop. The wind was blowing hard but it was right down the runway. We could see the soybeans bending in the breeze. We taxied to the fuel pump and Al, of Five Lakes Aviation, met and fueled us ($4.08). It was a very nice facility nestled in a beautiful area of five lakes. Al offered us a car and invited us to stay. All of which reminds me to say: small airports tout their communities; they are good for business. I would ask all 'city fathers' to appreciate that. Inside Five Lakes Aviation, some crop dusters-- one who had lived in Albany, Oregon, near our home --were studying their fields on a computer screen. So *that's* how they do that these days! We were bent on making more miles toward home on our first day so we took off for our next stop: Mitchell, South Dakota.

I regretted not being able to stay at Fairmont. As we flew away, I looked back over the right wing and there was a lovely little town surrounded by five lakes. There were old historic-looking buildings and I knew that there was character in this town. And maybe a few characters too. A trip for another day.

Even at 6500' MSL the outside air temperature was near 90F. The oil temp rose and sat on 200F. Normal is around 180F. Hot days are harder on engines-- but that's why they're tough, right? Even from altitude we could see the crops bending in the breeze. Does the wind *always* blow in the Midwest?

Mitchell Municipal (MHE) had a choice of runways so we picked the one that was mostly lined up with the wind. We landed and taxied to the gas pump. Mickey, a young A&P working on his flying ratings, met and fueled us ($4.65). The FBO was Wright Brothers

Aviation Ltd., their motto, 'Making Flights "Wright."' Their aircraft tug was a nicely restored 1946 Farmall "M" tractor. Now, you can't beat that with a stick! That evening the weather channel forecast nasty thunderstorms for the night and next day. (Did I ever tell you how much I hate red blotches moving across a TV weather map?) I called Mickey from the motel and asked if there was a hangar available. He said, "Sure. It's $25.00 a night." I said, "Put 'er in there." That night the sky cracked and roared and lightening flashed and it rained waterfalls and I slept like a baby knowing our airplane was warm and dry. It stormed all the next day, too, so we stayed put. Those two days of hangar fees were the best $50.00 I ever spent. The next morning dawned with clear skies so we left our friends at Mitchell and took off for our next fuel stop: Rapid City, South Dakota.

Mitchell, by the way, is the home of the Corn Palace. If you don't know that I would be surprised. Everyone knows about the Corn Palace. They are quite proud of it. We stayed at the very nice Holiday Inn in Mitchell and for two days watched the rain and wind and listened to the thunder, and wondered if we would ever get back to Oregon. We didn't exactly experience the hardships of, say, the wagon trains, but being at the mercy of the weather took patience. The folks at Wright Bros. lobby greeted us warmly in the morning sun and helped us roll our dry airplane out of their pristine hangar, glad to help us along our way.

I know, I know….Rapid City (RAP) has a control tower. It was the one exception on the trip to our 'uncontrolled airport rule.' We landed there because it was on a straight line past Mt. Rushmore, which we wanted to see, to our next stop. And, yeah, the airport did not have the ambiance to which we had become accustomed. There was just too much bustle and such: tower chatter, turn here, hold there, let the airliner go by, yakety-yak. Nice enough place, nice enough people, but not our cup of tea, know what I mean? We're into people, not bustle. Bustle was in another life; our new life is 'uncontrolled.' We got fuel ($4.39), got the Mt. Rushmore frequency and left. Next stop: Riverton, Wyoming.

We flew past Mt. Rushmore-- pretty neat --enroute to Riverton. My spotter once again said, "Airplane!" Yup, Cessna, opposite direction, about 500' above us. Busy place, Rushmore. Crossing into Wyoming there is a noticeable decrease in radio chatter on CTAF, mostly because there is a noticeable decrease in the number of airports under you. What you see on the sectional instead is a tiny black square that says "ranch." I thought to myself, 'I guess I'll head for the "ranch" if the engine quits; it's either that or spend the night with the coyotes.' I became totally tuned to engine sounds: 100 FPM up sounds different than 100 FPM down. It became bumpy again in the afternoon but Riverton was just ahead-- another adventure into the unknown.

Riverton (RIW) had only moderate winds. That was a welcome change. We landed and a nice lady, Wanda, parked and fueled us ($4.49). We asked of a courtesy car. Wanda said, "It's in the shop but you can take that one over there" and pointed to where her daughter, Michelle, and dog, Brandy, were washing a car. Once again, another bright spot with good people at 'small airport' America. And, besides that, when I walked into the FBO, there was a *Sport Aviation* on top of the magazine pile on the coffee table. I like this place, Jim's Aircraft Service, a lot! We stayed in a motel downtown that still had the type of key that you can drop in a mailbox. That evening we had an adult beverage in the rustic bar. On a chalkboard behind the bartender was written, "Riverton, 9th largest city, 9817; total population of state, 507,000." I asked the bartender, "Does that answer most of the questions you get asked?" He said, "Pretty much."

The next morning an antelope crossed the road as we drove to the airport. At the airport we got to meet Jim, Wanda's husband. He and Brandy sat and talked with us a while and we spoke of some of the politics of running a small airport operation. We thought that they do it very well. We thanked him and set about towards our next stop: Burley, Idaho.

Riverton had a nice western feel to it. There are elk heads mounted on walls and lots of brochures on the Tetons and Yellowstone national parks. It was the kind of city you stayed in when you were a child on a 'car vacation' with your folks. Knowing we were heading over the mountains the next morning, we did some concentrated flight planning, then had a steak dinner and climbed into bed by 7:30 pm.

We left Riverton and began the climb over the *big* mountains, well, actually, *through* them. They were, once again, beautiful and forbidding. But, also once again, our little airplane answered the call and just kept purring along. We flew past Yellowstone, over Jackson

Hole and through the Tetons again. Crossing Idaho Falls, Idaho the ground flattened. Subtly, that's a good feeling for a pilot. We skirted a line of developing thunderstorms and made a beeline to Burley, Idaho. We were *sensing* home now.

Landing at Burley (BYI) was a blast from the past. Again, there was not a soul on the ramp. I walked into a big, quonset-type hangar. A man was playing solitaire on the computer and there were a bunch of cats about. Too, there were a bunch of shirttails with names and dates on them hanging on one wall. It was good to see because you hardly see that anymore. A nice lady drove the fuel truck up to our airplane and said, "We'll give you twenty cents off a gallon if you fuel yourself." I fueled myself ($4.09). We didn't stay long because we were getting 'itchy.' Next stop: Home.

It is difficult to describe the special bonding that took place on this adventure. We were two, in the skies in our trusted plane, sailing over treacherous terrain, exploring a new world. I watched the back of Lauran's head for hours, admiring his abilities, trusting him to get us back home. He impressed me more than ever, with his patience, his rigid planning and execution. If I had any fear of flying, he knew how to ease that fear in me. As we flew those last hours over the mountains towards home, I knew this trip would sustain me for a lifetime. I hated to see it end and couldn't wait to get home both at the same time.

The last leg was our longest at three and one-half hours but the weather was good, the winds favorable, the territory familiar and I'd still have a strong forty-five minutes of fuel at destination. So we 'pressed on' through some bumps and haze from forest fires but mostly good air. As we approached central Oregon, we could see the outlines of Mt. Jefferson and Mt. Hood in the Cascade mountain range. Home, by golly, home! Kay took a picture of the mountains, the reflection in the canopy showing my occasionally used portable Garmin GPS III Pilot.

We passed between Mt. Jefferson and Mt. Hood and let down towards our home airport in Salem, Oregon (SLE). The wind was strong down the runway but the landing was the best of the trip. We whooped and hollered. It is difficult to express the elation we felt from accomplishing our goal. After we parked, my bride kissed the ground; I kissed her and then hugged the airplane. Mission accomplished;

adventure completed.   We had experienced 'good America' in a homebuilt airplane. It was grand!

Thanks to small town and small airport America! Your faces, smiles and generosity inspired us.

41

HOT DOG

This is an addendum to our story about "Small Airport America" in the February 2007 issue of Sport Aviation. It's an addendum I want to share with you. About mid-way through the article, while talking about our experience at Sheldon Regional Airport in Sheldon, Iowa, my bride mentioned, *"Three old faded enamel lawn chairs-- red, yellow, and blue --were lined up by the hangar. Empty now."*

Kari called from Sheldon and told me about those chairs.

Those were Hotdog's chairs.

Hotdog's real name is Elmer Denhartog. From Sheldon, Elmer was a B-24 turret gunner in WWII. On a bombing mission over Germany, one bomb stuck in the rack, refusing to fall. The young pilot-in-command said, "We're going to have to land with it."

Elmer said, "No. We're not." And with that he proceeded to where the bomb was and kicked the bomb. Nothing. He kicked it some more. Nothing. He kicked it a *lot* more. And a lot more after that. The bomb gave......and fell. After that, his crew gave him the name "Hotdog." It stuck. For life.

While kicking the bomb, Hotdog got frostbite. For the frostbite, he was awarded the Purple Heart. Hotdog chuckled when he told the story. How is it that true heroes are so modest?

You've probably already noticed that I've been speaking of Hotdog in the past tense. Hotdog's gone now. Age eighty-two. Heart attack. More on that later; there's a story there, too.

Hotdog came home to Sheldon after the war and made his living as a trucker. He married June and they raised four children, two boys and two girls. Through it all, aviation was once and forever a part of Hotdog's life. In his later years he was a fixture at the Sheldon airport. A beloved fixture. Sometimes he'd arrive at 7:30 AM and not leave until 9:00 PM. He built and flew airplanes and helped others build airplanes. And the stories flowed. Camaraderie flowed. A way of life flowed: grass roots aviation with heart.

Hotdog found the chairs and painted them himself. He put them outside his hangar. It was there, especially in the evenings, that he would sit and sip a beer. And they came. His many friends. People from town. And they would sit and watch and talk and soak up the last rays of sunshine from the day and then the warmth of the evening. They would come to sit with Hotdog and listen and share and solve problems and otherwise experience the joy of loving life. Life at its best.

Then the heart attack. December 7, 2005. It was unexpected. In good health, Hotdog was still flying right up to his last days. But life is imperfect. Kari, from the FBO, and Chad were there when it happened….at the airport. Hotdog was taken to the hospital. One of the physicians who treated him had taken flying lessons at Sheldon and, of course, knew Hotdog. People from the airport went to the hospital to see him. The hospital said, "Family only."

June said, "The people at the airport are family." The hospital let them in the room. Hotdog passed away among friends.

The guys at the airport now look after June, check on her and shovel her snow and such. That's what "family" does.

Time marches on. The old FBO building at the airport is being torn down. A new one is being built. The people at the airport are saving Hotdog's chairs for the new building. Others will sit in them and do what Hotdog inspired them to do: enjoy life, enjoy each day, share, give and laugh. Too, Hotdog's hat still hangs on a nail by the door. His hat will also be saved.

Hotdog was a regular at Oshkosh…..even before it was Oshkosh. He attended when the "fly-in" was at Rockford. And all the years thereafter. He especially loved Patty Wagstaff's routine. It is said that she knew him by name. She'd taxi by and there would be an older gentleman, year after year, waving his hat. And Patty would say, "There's Hotdog!"

Let's reflect on all of the above for a minute: small airports aren't just small airports. They're a way of life, held together by passion and the common bond of airplanes. And people like Hotdog.

Thanks, Hotdog, for keeping the spirit alive.

42

GREEN LAKE

Okay, let's talk about it: Green Lake. Specifically, Green Lake, WI on July 23, 2006 --the day before AirVenture officially began-- at 10:00 am. And 11:00 am. And 11:30 am. I was there, circling, for that hour and a half. Along with about one-hundred twenty-five others of you. We all went round-and-round. And round-and-round some more. Each of you has a story to tell that probably mirrors mine. That's why I'm telling it here....for all of us.

Green Lake on that day and at that time was --and these are strong words-- borderline chaos. At the very least it was a gaggle with a capital "G." But, ya know, it all worked out, as such things usually do with patience and people working together. There were a couple exceptions to "people working together"-- we'll talk about those a little later. (There are *always* exceptions, aren't there?)

We started the day from Prairie du Chien, WI. At RV-8 cruise speeds it's only about thirty minutes to Oshkosh and almost on a straight line for a direct entry into the hold --if needed(!) --at Green Lake. I liked the "straight line" to destination because I wanted to get there with gas to spare. (Little did I know how much I would need that "gas to spare.") It was an idyllic beginning. As we were leaving the nice airport and nice people at Prairie du Chien, a group of seven Champs arrived. I reckoned that after they got fuel they were headed to the same place we were. Cool! Enroute to Oshkosh the air was smooth and the scenery grand. I told my bride it was a lot like going into combat: quiet, each to his/her own thoughts, calm, but knowing that something very different was up ahead. Out of the corner of my eye I could see my bride holding her arms up to one side of the canopy. I asked, "What are you doing?"

She laughed, "I'm practicing holding up my HBP (Home Built Parking) sign for the ground guides. It's my only job and I want to do it right."

I listened to the arrival ATIS. It sounded busy, as in "expect holds." I tuned in the arrival frequency (Fisk Approach) and, sure enough, it *was* busy. The situation ahead began coming into view. I spotted Green Lake as depicted on the AirVenture Arrival NOTAM. And then, as I got closer still, I spotted what looked to be a swarm of locusts.....only these locusts were airplanes! By some stroke of luck, with a quick left and right, I was able to slide in the hold in trail behind a blue and white Cessna. I was in! I was at OSH! Well, almost. I felt like calling like you do when reporting in trail formation, "Four's in." But I would have had to call, "One-hundred twenty-five's in."

So there we were, all at ninety knots (sort of) and 1800' MSL (sort of). We were all dressed up (sort of) but with no place to go-- there had been an accident at Wittman Regional. To their credit, I suppose, the controllers didn't say much about the accident, only that there had been some runway closures and "things are backed up...please be patient." Pilots understand that perfectly and we all work our way through such things in our own way. But there remained the problem of getting a lot of airplanes on the ground. Life has a way of marching on. It's not right; it's not wrong; it just *is*.

Finally the controllers were saying, "The Rush Lake and Green Lake patterns appear full. (I wanted to say, "You should see them from up here!") Oshkosh arriving aircraft outside these patterns, find someplace to hold and hold until we get the patterns cleared out." Hold "someplace?" That's pretty free-wheeling. It's kinda like saying, "Good luck!" In my other (airline) life I've held at Los Angeles, Seattle, San Francisco, Denver and such but I always had my very own racetrack and no one within one-thousand feet, either above or below. Now I was holding with one-hundred twenty-five others in the same racetrack at the same altitude! My bride, knowing I've been flying for forty years, asked, "Ever seen anything like this before?"

Answer, "Nope. Never," as I stuck like glue to my blue and white Cessna lead. But, ya know, I love aviation's challenges and this was one of them. There was no time, in my hour and a half at Green Lake, that I didn't have seven to ten aircraft visible in my canopy windscreen. (It's no wonder transponders are on standby at OSH-- a controller's radar scope would look like the Fourth of July if they weren't.)

As the airport began to open up again there came the matter of spacing. The controllers kept saying, "We need half mile spacing. We can't release you to the airport until we have it." Makes sense, right? You just can't turn a gaggle of five airplanes at Fisk to the 36 L/R arrival at Wittman and expect the tower to sort them out. You just can't; there's no time. But spacing --especially "self-spacing"-- is sometimes easier said than done. Put four fish swimming in a gallon jar and they can space nicely; put fifty fish in that same jar and spacing becomes more difficult. We needed to circle Lake Winnebago to get spacing on July 23, 2006 at 10:00 am. And 11:00 am. And 11:30 am.

The controllers would occasionally throw in a pep-talk, "Welcome to Oshkosh. We know it's busy. Just be patient and we'll get you in so you can enjoy the show." The 'Pink Shirts' (controllers) were painting 'The Big Picture.' Good for them!

Then "The Exception" raised his ugly head and it was always the same voice, "Fisk, you need to tell the Cherokee to widen his hold."

Answer (thinking to myself): No, the controller's job is to tell you *to* hold, not *how* to hold.

Same voice again, "Fisk, there's people holding inside our hold."

Answer: Same answer as above.

"Fisk, there's airplanes going over our head."

Answer: Yes, per the NOTAM, the one-hundred thirty-five knot hold is 500' above you.

"Fisk, if I don't get in soon, I'll have to divert. I've been holding over two hours."

Answer: Yes, you will. And that's *your* decision to make, not the controller's.

All the while this guy is complaining, he's tying up the frequency and keeping the controllers from being able to do their job. Some nerves began to fray with, "Quiet!" And, "Just hold!" And, finally, "Shut up!"

Am I stepping on some toes here? Maybe. But so be it. I've never been fond of pilots at busy airports who think they're the only airplane in the sky. They just "fry my bacon."

Gradually, as they said they would, the controllers cleared the lower and then the upper Rush Lake holding patterns and made mention that some "Green Lake people" could make their way to Fisk but with the admonition "as long as you have half mile spacing." I was headed that direction and *thinking* that direction. My Cessna ahead turned left to go around the hold again. Space! I kept going straight ahead, up the tracks (the pink paint on the tracks was a very nice touch) toward Fisk. As I approached what I thought was Fisk --it's not exactly a metropolis but Rush Lake was unmistakably off to the left-- the controller, in one breath, said, "Canard, turn left, continue the hold, RV (that's me!) turn right, follow the Bonanza." As soon as I heard the "r" in "right" I was in an eighty degree bank toward Wittman. The controller said, "Good!" Then he said, "Monitor tower." I then got to rock my wings like I'd practiced at home. Way cool!

I monitored tower and followed the Bonanza for the 36 L/R arrival. Except, all of a sudden, the Bonanza turned *away* from the airport, going I know not where. I eventually lost sight of him in the ground clutter. Why'd he do that? Don't know! So I keyed the mic with, "RV's on left base...Bonanza's not in sight."

Tower said, "RV, cleared to land 36L...make short approach." Then he came back with, "RV, land beyond the third intersection." (Basically, that's the pink dot.)

I answer, "RV, roger." I added a tad of power and a few seconds later we plunked down on 36L. OSH at last!

We taxied off the runway and my bride held up her HBP sign. (Practice makes perfect!) The 'Orange Vest' volunteers then took over and, in their excellent manner, directed us in. As we taxied down P1, the side barriers came up, people stopped and looked, took pictures and we, giddy, laughed and waved. The Green Lake conquerors had arrived!

We were then further directed to our parking spot on row 315. As we shut down and I rolled back the canopy my bride let out a whoop and a holler. The earpieces on my headset expanded according to the decibels coming from the rear seat as the sound reverberated from eardrum to eardrum. The volunteers and crew of "Diamond Di" parked next to us (Mike and Diane, we learned later) all laughed and asked, "First time to Oshkosh?"

My bride answered, "First time to *fly* here."

A nice touch a while later was that two guys came walking down row 315, recognized our airplane, stopped, pointed at us and said, "You! You were my wingman! Nice job." They turned out to be Tim and Mike, and were flying the blue and white Cessna that I followed for an hour and a half. It was a flying club Cessna 182 from Hillsboro, OR, which is about forty miles up the road from our home. And thus began the 'people connections' that makes AirVenture so great.

That afternoon we talked to several other RV pilots and asked, "Come in today?"

"Yeah."

"What time?"

"About three."

"Any problems?"

"Nope. Just sailed on in."

Some people miss all the fun.

43

CONNECTIONS

EAA AirVenture at Oshkosh is fertile ground for pilots. There are airplanes, aviation innovation, air shows, like-minded people and…..connections. You know about the airplanes; you can see the innovation by walking the grounds; you can watch the air shows; you can strike up an aviation conversation with anyone on the grounds. The connections, however, generally happen more subtly, in visits here and there, often in the evening over dinner or around a campfire at Camp Scholler. I find them both fascinating and heartwarming.

Early one day during the show a friend came up to me and said, "Wow! I was walking with a buddy of mine and his dad. The buddy gravitated toward the 0-1 Bird Dogs because he had flown them in Vietnam. And one of the Bird Dogs was one that had been in his squadron in Vietnam. Then we all walked toward the Wildcats and there was one that my buddy's dad had flown. Only at Oshkosh!" Yup, "only at Oshkosh," where connections routinely meet.

That same evening, my USAF pilot training buddy, "Foghorn," invited my bride and me to his motor home for hamburgers (in the shape of the State of Texas) and a toddy. Also visiting him was his college roommate, Jerry. That's the set-up so you can imagine the conversations: lots of talk about old times. And that's a fun way to spend an evening. "Foghorn" told lies about me and I told lies about him. I laughed a lot listening to "Foghorn" and Jerry talking about their college days, like jumping over trash cans on their bikes. And Jerry talking about "Foghorn" being boisterous (hence the name) even then. (Okay, truth be known, "Foghorn's" a boisterous pussycat; he'd give you the shirt off his back.) And Jerry talking about his early flying lessons, when his instructor said, "Watch this!" The instructor raised the nose of the Swift on takeoff, retracted the gear and all Jerry remembers is the slap-slap-slap of the prop on the pavement just before they bellied-in off the end of the runway. Nobody hurt; flight instructor ego bruised; airplane (it belonged to Jerry) repairable. The rest of the story? Jerry still flies and still loves Swifts.

Jerry is an engineer by trade, worked for General Motors for years. But always the thinker, he tinkered with 'things aviation' in his off time. Turns out-- and here's the connection --he manufactured something that is in the magneto of my airplane. I'd never have known had we not spent the evening with "Foghorn" and Jerry in Oshkosh. So here's what "Foghorn" did: he opened a bottle of fifteen year old Scotch. We all took a sip and signed the box the bottle came in. Next year, who ever is there gets to sip-and-sign, too. We'll do that each year until it's gone…or we're gone. From connections come traditions.

Follow me closely on this next story; it's a circuitous road. Before we left for Oshkosh we promised our two Grandsons, ages six and four, that, when we got back, we'd take them to Yellowstone National Park in the motor home. Before we left for Oshkosh, we started making reservations for the Yellowstone trip. One place where we made a reservation was the Longhorn RV Park in Dubois, Wyoming. On the website was a tab labeled THE OWNERS. My bride checked the tab and then hollered for me to come see what she found. The owners, Art and Charlotte, were proud EAA members and owned a Grizzly Cub. That's one connection. Charlotte wrote back and said they were also going to Oshkosh. That's another connection. We then gave her the number of our camping spot at Oshkosh. A couple days after we arrived at AirVenture there appeared a note at our campsite from Art and Charlotte, "We're one block south of the intersection of Stits and Elm. Stop by."

These people are strangers, right? But I've never had a bad experience meeting anyone at Oshkosh. So after we left "Foghorn's", we found Art and Charlotte's place. Connection complete. But here's the rest of the deal: Art and Charlotte turned out to be really special people. They're accomplished, unassuming and passionate about aviation, my kind of people. Long story short, Art sold his part of the big wheat farm in South Dakota-- a life he grew up with --and bought the motor home park, a beautiful place on the Wind River, with longhorn cattle in the pasture as you drive in. He's been involved in aviation for a long time and is very savvy about the mountain flying he does in Wyoming. Flying completes Art. He says, "I can't imagine my life without it." Charlotte is a practicing MD, also a pilot, and has been involved with the EAA, through her Dad, since she was ten years old. As they said, "I can't imagine not being at Oshkosh when the show is happening." So here's what they do every year: they bring what they call "The AirVenture Support Vehicle." It's a forty-two foot fifth-wheel trailer, full of everything you need for a week at Oshkosh. Accordingly, many were gathered around their campfire when we stopped by. So....more connections.

Earlier in the day I had watched the "Heritage Flight'" fly-by. It's one of my favorite parts of the show: classic airplanes flown by pilots with a passion for flight, history on display, heritage and freedom on parade against the backdrop of a clear blue sky. America proud! I gives me chills and I love it and honor it. This day there was a P-51, a P-38, an F-86 and an A-10. At Art and Charlotte's campfire a guy in a flight suit comes up to me and asks, "Are you Lauran Paine?" I said, "I am." He said, "I read your stuff and I really like it." His name? Paul. His job? Flying the A-10 for the "Heritage Flight." I said, "No. It is I that admire you." Paul is a fine young man, the type that makes you proud of our military. Very proud. And thankful for them, too. Paul's connection with Art and Charlotte? He wanted bigger bush wheels for his personal airplane, a Cessna 180, so, seeing Art's Grizzly Cub, traded tires with Art. Art was happy; Paul was happy. The aviation world is a small one, especially at Oshkosh for one week a year.

As promised, after we got home from Oshkosh, we piled the Grandsons into the motor home and headed for Yellowstone. After our visit we took the south exit, drove past the Grand Tetons and went to the Longhorn RV Park in Dubois, Wyoming and stayed at Art and Charlotte's place. Wonderful country, clean air, wonderful people. That morning, Art had flown the Grizzly Cub and had spotted three grizzly bears. Another connection.

I smile to think of all the connections that are made during the one week of AirVenture. Aviation is a thread that runs through some mighty fine people.

44

AMMETERS

This is a tale of two ammeters. Make that three ammeters. Before I begin, however, I'm going to tell you up front that I don't like ammeters: they're stupid. Either that or I'm stupid. I'll leave that judgment to you.

There's something else you need to know: electricity and I are barely on speaking terms. I don't speak "electron" well and the electrons I know are patently unresponsive when I rant and rave at them. Let's just say that we're at an 'electrical standoff.'

Electrons go hither and yon, want to be routed, grounded, crimped and even connected to the correct locations. They're very demanding of knowledge I generally don't have. Worse, sometimes they hide. There'll be 12 volts worth of them going to one location and then they'll disappear at the next location. Again, I rant and rave and they do not respond. They are supposed to do what I understand they're supposed to do. Know what I mean? They're supposed to come out of the battery, go where they're supposed to go, do what they're supposed to do and, engine running, the alternator will run stuff and even put electrons back into the battery. To me it's EWOD (Either Works Or Doesn't).

Back to ammeters. I installed one in my RV-8. It's right next to the voltmeter. I like voltmeters. If you have volts, they register. If the alternator's running, they register more. If not, they don't. It's a simple-- and reliable --concept. But not ammeters. They're fickle. And weird. We flew our RV-8 to AirVenture and back last summer and the ammeter seemed to work fine: a little discharge (-) with the battery on and a little charge (+) with the engine running. Nice ammeter. Yeah, right.

On about the third flight at home after returning from AirVenture, as I taxied in, I noticed a large needle swing out of the corner of my eye. It was my 'friend' the ammeter. The needle had swung and pegged itself to the plus side of the gauge. I mulled, "What the heck?" When I shut down, the needle went to the middle, 'zero' position. I flicked the master switch back on and the needle pegged again. Master off, needle back to zero.

Okay, okay. I can picture you now sitting in your favorite chair reading this and you already know what the problem is, don't you? I don't like you. You're fifty times smarter than I am and I'm sensitive about my stupidity. But, for the other two people in the EAA who are as dumb as I am, I'm going to continue.

Back in the hangar, into the cockpit I crawl with a couple screwdrivers, a flashlight and voltmeter. I know that I will have forgotten something and will have to crawl back out of the cockpit and get it. I also know that I will have to do this at least five times. I remove the instrument panel and lay it face down in my lap. I need a different screwdriver. It's in the toolbox. I crawl out of the cockpit, get the screwdriver and crawl back in. That's one. Visually, all the wires seem to be in order. I know every one of them because I installed them. I checked all the connections. They checked good. I even looked at the shunt. There are wires from it to the ammeter. The shunt is there not because I know what it does but because the instructions said to put it there. All the shunt connections were good, too. I then resorted to my standard, fall-back position: wiggling. I wiggled everything. I'm good at wiggling.

Convinced that I had now tamed the mutant electron, I propped the instrument panel up on my lap and turned on the master switch. The ammeter needle pegged to the right. Again. Still. The score remained: Electricity, 1, Lauran, 0.

Okay, it was time to go public and ask the wandering airport intelligentsia. Asking can be risky because the more electrically inclined speak in 'tongue.' They use words like "ohm" and "positive" and "negative" and "spike" and "surge" and "short" and "resistance." I am usually reduced to nodding and smiling. Ken made the most sense to me with, "Take the dang thing out and put a happy-face in its place."

I finally decided it was the gauge itself. Not because I knew, only because I had no other answer to my ammeter dilemma. So I removed the gauge and the gauge and I drove to Van's. (It's nice that they're close by). Terrified of being wrong while smack in the middle of the den of 'the keepers of all RV knowledge' I stepped up to the counter and plopped down the gauge . My friend and Van's employee

Rob walked over. I pointed and said, as convincingly as I could, "The gauge is bad."

Rob immediately threw down the gauntlet with, "Naw, the gauge is good. It's probably installation error." I've known Rob a long time; I'd be disappointed if he didn't flick me some guff. He didn't disappoint.

I stick to my guns with, "No, the gauge is bad." And add for emphasis, "Bad, bad, bad." I was trying to cover my doubts with bravado.

Rob said, "I'll check it." With that he left with my ammeter gauge. I was left standing on pins and needles. Rob returned and, looking down, mumbled, "Gauge is bad."

"YESSSSSSS!!!!!"

But you know what? Rob knew it was bad the minute I set it on the counter. How? Because with no power to the gauge the needle was at the 'zero' position; the needle should be resting on the peg that is there for it to rest on when the power is off, which is way over at the -40 position. The gauge had 'slipped a cog' (my layman's description) and was reading 40 amps off. Rob gave me a new gauge.

Is that was you thought it was all along? No? Okay, I like you again.

The third ammeter gauge? It's on my Dad's 1953 Ford tractor that I'm restoring. Well, it is now, anyway. For the first forty or so years that we owned the tractor, it didn't have an ammeter, only the hole where it was supposed to go. Tractor ran fine. Until I restored it. I installed a new battery, wiring, regulator, points, plugs and…..an ammeter. I started the tractor. It ran good but the ammeter, you guessed it, registered nothing. My bias arose and I said, "Stupid ammeter!" Those 'in the know' told me that since I had disconnected all the electricity during restoration that I had to "polarize" the generator. What??!!?? Touch a jumper wire from the BATT position on the voltage regulator to the GEN position. Whatever! But I did it to appease the electron gods. On start up, still nothing from the ammeter. I tested the generator with my multi-meter. Nothing. Generator was bad. So that's why we had to charge the battery so often the last few years! (My Dad was a disciple of EWOD, too.) The nice ammeter was trying to tell me something. I put on a new generator. Ammeter's now happy. Demanding…….but happy.

Okay, there you have it. Throw me to the wolves in your electrical classes. I can take it. I may be stupid but at least I'm stubborn.

The happy ending? Me and my ammeters are all happy.......for now.

45

BECAUSE WE FLY

I have never envied another profession. Admired? Yes. Respected? Yes. But envied? No. Why? Because I fly. By my way of thinking, flying scratches a lot of life's itches.

Flying is all I ever wanted to do and, except for a couple short knockdowns and detours along the byways of life, it's pretty much all I've ever done. I was briefly intrigued by a career in medicine. It was for the intellectual thrill of the chase for a cure. And I love to farm the land-- still do --but aviation is and always has been both my profession and my passion. And…..no regrets.

But there's more to flying than just *doing* flying. There is what flying does to you. First of all, you can't fly without having a strong work ethic. You can't learn to fly by humming at the feet of a guru. You have to study, learn, practice, make mistakes, get bounced, bumped, iced up, maybe even yelled at and then do it all over again until you get it right. And there's no substitute for doing it right. Do it right or get hurt, that's how it works. *After* all that, however, there is the reward that comes with accomplishing something challenging: satisfaction.

There's something else about flying, too: you don't have to do it for a living to experience the passion. You have only to get out there and *do* it and the passion will surround you.

It's intellectually satisfying. Thinking and planning and flying so as to arrive at minimums on approach with all the needles centered and the airplane configured to land safely in ½ mile and blowing snow…..that's *very* satisfying. To push the throttles forward on takeoff and experience all the engineering and science in your airplane, that gives you faith in your fellow man. And to know that you always have to be *aware*. After all, when you're flying, something is always changing. It teaches you to take nothing for granted, either in flying or in life. To

198

watch the ground fall away from you while you ride silver wings aloft is little more than physics but gives meaning to life because you *feel* alive while doing it.

I never feel the need to tailgate on a freeway or to swerve in and out of lanes passing cars to show my worth. My airplane gives me speed to satisfy. And I never feel the need to go on a carnival ride for stimulus. My airplane gives it to me.

And flying, we can do these things, too. Fly supersonic, above 50,000 ft. and over the North Pole. Fly celebrities and elderly ladies (I prefer to fly elderly ladies). Fly in combat and appreciate our country. Fly during sunrises and sunsets and see vistas from higher than the highest mountains. Meet people at small airports who work hard, give much and ask for little. I once flew a middle age lady who had never met her biological Mom.....to meet her biological Mom. The circumstance was not my concern, only the connection. I watched the lady nervously wrap a Kleenex tissue around two fingers of her left hand, over and over. Then, after we parked, I watched out my cockpit window as an older lady, leaning on the three feet high chain link fence, saw her daughter and her daughter saw her and they KNEW. They'd never met but they KNEW. These things are all a part of me because I fly.

And, in the air, we can twist and turn and roll and loop and the earth becomes our playground. And fly formation with our friends with trust and discipline and practiced skill. And we can go to fly-ins and strike up a conversation with anyone and be on common ground.

I have flown around thunderstorms-- some seemingly bigger than the sky --and through ice. Somehow, also satisfying. And I have flown when it is crystal clear and smooth as glass, all the while marveling at the machine, the sky and the vistas. And have been able to share that with my most important person, my bride of 38 years. All because I fly.

And I have met and made friends with people who share the passion. Lifelong friends. Friends who I would do anything for and they for me. I like them because they have a work ethic, values and passion, the things that made America and aviation great. I've come across a couple creeps, too, but they are definitely in the minority. High standards are what aviation is about.

I've had engine failures, near misses and done a couple of stupid things....and survived. All of which taught me the value of training, and that life isn't all about blame but about living the best you know how with what you have. All these things because I fly.

And I have built an airplane and flown it across this great land. I am thankful for that freedom and am willing to fight for it.

And I am proud of others who fly….supplies, sick people and Young Eagles. These things happen because *they* fly.

And, bottom line, we all share these things because *we* fly. The bond is far reaching and strong. With this magazine I know I am preaching to the choir. And the choir *knows* what I'm saying because they've been there…in flight. All the more reason to sing out: "Come fly with me and you will see; that in the blue you'll be happy, too."

How many other professions/passions offer all these things?

I have to add this: the future is bright for those who have a good work ethic and a desire to work in aviation. For those who are working to acquire ratings during the down times, they will be ready and hired when the good times return. And, make no mistake, they will return. For as long as we have gas, air travel remains the fastest way to get you where you're going. Are there problems from time to time with air travel? Sure. No type of transportation is immune from problems. Got three days? Travel by train. Got three aspirin? Travel the Los Angeles or Washington, DC freeways at 5:00 PM. It's an imperfect world.

Or do it this way: work the good job and rent, buy or build an airplane. (I'm partial to building; you get to touch your passion every day.) Flying a private airplane is one of the last great freedoms. Experience it.

I dreamed about aviation as a child, did it as an adult and now I play at it. It's been a good ride. Am I rich? No. Famous? No. Happy? Yes.

My sincere wish is that many young people will follow where we, the older, have tread-- like we followed when we were young --and experience the joy and passion of aviation. The journey is satisfying, rewarding, fun and it's quite likely that you'll never envy another way of life.

46

MILESTONE

Indulge me, please. I recently passed an aviation milestone of sorts.

It was July 11th-- my birthday. Seven-eleven. The year was 1967. I was twenty-two, going on twenty-three years old. And I was in U.S. Air Force pilot training at Webb AFB, Texas and on the scheduling board for two "area acro solo" flights in the T-38. I was where I worked for twenty-two years to be and doing exactly what I wanted to be doing. And today I was going to be doing it alone in a cobalt blue sky in an airplane that knows few limits. Happy birthday.

I can still remember the sequence: check the schedule board and get the tail number and the row were the airplane was parked. There was no ignition key to get; it would be ready when you walked up to it. At the allotted time, you would go to the equipment room, slap your g-suit around you and zip it up, throw your parachute on your back, grab your helmet, oxygen mask, kneeboard and gloves, check your oxygen mask at the test station on the way out the door then walk into the sunshine. There was a tram to shuttle you to your airplane but I usually just walked if the airplane wasn't parked in 'the north-forty.' I liked the walk-- I was a knight, suited up and marching to my steed. (Gimme some slack here: I was only twenty-three, remember?) At the very least, it was my time to get into character to strap on my mini-rocket ship. I *loved* the anticipation.

There it sat, on "G" row, tail #834: sleek, proud, powerful and fast. I was thinking, "You and me, buddy. Let's defy gravity in every axis." Acknowledge the crew chief (they are, after all, the ones who keep these airplanes flyable), check the Maintenance Log, pre-flight, pull gear pins and ejection seat safety pins, and finish fastening your parachute. Then climb up the ladder and settle into the seat. SETTLE INTO THE SEAT! This is home; this is happiness; this is adventure. The airplane surrounds you. You connect to it: to the ejection seat, plug into the g-suit and oxygen systems, and strap on your kneeboard and pull on your gloves. Then run the checklist-- caress the switches, throttles and stick. The anticipation builds. Then you pull on your helmet, slap on the oxygen mask and lower the helmet visor to mute the sun. Then you raise your gloved hand and give a little twirl of two fingers to signal the crew chief: starting engines. Push the start switch, advance the throttle to idle at 14% RPM, and watch that the EGT doesn't climb past 890 degrees. You can *feel* it; your steed is coming alive. Then you do the same thing again for the left engine. Then you put your fists together, thumbs out, and pull your fists apart: pull the chocks. Then the crew chief out front raises his arms and motions you forward. Power up, the jet moves. You roll forward a little then check the brakes. Tap them firmly and bounce the nose strut a little-- it's just *so* cool to do that.

Taxi to the run-up area, run more checklists and, after being cleared onto the runway, check mil (100%) power: this horse wants to *run*. You're cleared for takeoff-- for more fun than a human being should be allowed to have. Canopy down/locked/light-out, power up, light the afterburners and it's a RACE!! Focus ahead; vision to the side is a blur. Rotate, positive rate, gear up, flaps up and pull the nose up. *Way* up. *Waaaay* up. And the ground falls rapidly away. At the top of the climb, roll inverted, let the nose come back to the horizon, roll upright and head to your practice area. Happy birthday.

Now for the next hour or so it's just you and your fighter, a match made in heaven. Loop. Straight up. Straight down. Split-S: straight down is *soooo* much fun. Immelman: from top to bottom, gain 10,000' and roll out on top of the world. Roll rapidly three times left, then one to the right-- to get your eyeballs centered again. Roll, pull, sweat, grunt-- this is joy personified. Twenty-three years old today. Thank you, Mom.

Back to the traffic pattern, up initial at 300 KIAS, pitch-out mid-field, haul the stick back, make the oxygen mask sag and the g-suit inflate and wing-tip vortices come off the wingtips. Do it with panache; fly it with spirit! Gear down, flaps. Fall "off the perch," 180 degree turn to final, and get "in the groove" on final at 155 KIAS. Plunk! Nose high for aerodynamic braking-- fun to do that! Then slow, clear the runway, raise the canopy, feel the breeze and taxi slowly back to "G" row to savor the experience. Park, shut down, listen to the engines whine down, get the 'chocks-in' signal, savor the ride some more then unhook and unbuckle and climb out. Sign the Maintenance

Log, "Flight O.K.," thank the crew chief and head back to the line shack. Happy birthday.

Now drink a bunch of water, eat a bag of peanuts and an hour or so later, do it all over again. Except, this time, go to "F" row and fly #594. Happy birthday, again.

Was I tired after all that? Not one iota. I was twenty three years old; I could have done that all day long. But tonight I had a dinner date with my girlfriend, Kay Lyn Statser. She gave me a present at dinner. It was a book, "The World's Fighting Planes," by William Green. Inside she inscribed, "To Lauran with love-- but be careful flying these things! Kay. 7/11/67."

It's now July 11, 2007-- forty years later, a milestone of sorts. It's also two careers-- one military and one airline --seven type ratings and nearly 20,000 hours later. It's also.....some really lousy weather, a couple near misses, four engine failures and a couple stupid things later, too. And my "fighter" is now piston powered-- an 0-360, to be exact --and I built it myself, an RV-8. I painted it military style. It completes me. It takes me back to where I started this aviation journey: sitting astraddle the airplane with a canopy overhead and a stick and throttle inside. And it is here that I *continue* to experience the joy of aviation. I've worked hard to be where I am but fully realize I've been propitious in genetics, lucky in the happenstance of life, and fortunate in marriage. And I give thanks for these things every day.

So, forty years later, July 11, 2007, it's time to commemorate the journey. The anticipation builds as I drive to the airport. There I open the hangar door and push my little fighter into the sunshine. It glints proudly. I preflight and climb in. I *settle* in. It's home-- airplane cockpits have always been home. But this one I designed and built myself; it is every inch what I want it to be. I strap-in, hearing the buckles snap. I like the sounds. They signal the beginning of the flight. I do the checklist, holler "Clear!" and start the engine. The airplane comes alive; I *feel* it come alive. I like it alive. I call for taxi and amble toward the runway. Ambling allows me to savor the experience. Cleared for takeoff, I roll: tail up, light on its wheels......airborne! Forty years later to the day. Not as high, not as fast, not as far, not as many g's, but with the *same* joy. *Still* the same joy. Aviation is a good life.

I climb on silvered wings and fly to my practice area. There I roll and loop and roll some more and remember the day forty years ago when I flew in kind. And somehow I also think of the pilots I've known who also loved the sky, who once touched it but now do not. My pilot training classmates: Steve, who is now recovering from a serious heart attack; Ken, who fell ill while flying 0-2's in Vietnam and now spends most of his days in a wheelchair; and Gary, who called everybody "Silly Savage," who now has a brain tumor. These rolls are for you guys, because you've been there and the sky will always be a part of you. And the loops, the climb, the top, the dive, the pull at the bottom, commemorative for Bruce, who hit the ground in an F-4, Guy who also hit the ground in another F-4 and Harold who did the same in an A-7. Did these guys want to die flying? Of course not. Did they want to be doing what they were doing? Yes, they did. And all of them once had "area acro solos" in the T-38 and there, I'm quite sure, felt the joy. They wanted to fly and fly they did. Their careers were shortened but their stars burned bright. I rolled and looped and looked at my wings in the air and thought of such things as I flew along forty years later. Bittersweet thoughts on a happy birthday.

I didn't want to land. I wanted to stay in the air and fly forever. But forever is not for mortals. So it was back to the traffic pattern for an overhead break to a landing and taxi-back, canopy open, to the hangar. Mixture to lean and the prop stopped. Switches off and I sat there. Just sat there.....for a long time. Time marches on but time is still good. And, yes, I'm thankful for that, too. Was I tired? A little--forty years later my 'abs' are a little more 'rounded,' there being forty more years of wear on the body. But the aviation joy is the same. Still the same. I climbed slowly out of the cockpit. I had another dinner date with Kay Lyn --now-- Paine, same girlfriend, forty years later. At dinner she gave me an Oregon State polo shirt: after family and flying, our other passion is college football. And a card. Well, actually, two cards. One card was inscribed, "Still loving you forever. Katie." The outside of the second card said, "It's your birthday! Get yer motor runnin'! Head out on the highway!" Inside it said, "Pick up bread and milk. Then come home again!" The inscription read, "Sometimes I crack myself up. Love you always-- Katie."

Aviation milestones are a time to reflect: reflect on the joy of aviation, the joy of life, the rewards of persistence, the fruit of hard work, on love and on another very happy birthday flying.

47

HONORING THE BROTHERHOOD

This is a story about a man, fair warning, beginning to end. A professional pilot. And about how his fellow pilots honored him.

First, some background: from time to time, I get letters from readers. It happens when you put lots of words on the pages of a magazine every month. Most all are quite nice and I've made friends with some wonderful people. And some-- fortunately very few --are not so nice. 'Tis the way of the world, something about "you can't please all of the people all of the time." (And I answer all my mail; if you didn't hear back from me, I didn't get your note.) BJ (initials) wrote me for a bit of a different reason. Oh, she wrote because she liked something I'd written, but mostly she wrote because we have the same last name. (Harry Paine, down Southern California way, who flies a Harmon Rocket, wrote me for much the same reason.) Payne with a "y' is the more common spelling; Paine with an "i" is much less common. I can trace my family's history to just before the Civil War-- I have my Great Grandfather's Civil War sword --but prior to that it gets a little murky. No matter, genealogy links or not, we Paine's became friends. And BJ's story touched me.

BJ Paine was married to Chuck Paine for fifty-seven years. Chuck was a professional pilot whose career spanned the heyday, including all the growing pains and ups and downs (no puns intended), of commercial aviation. His pilot certificate type ratings tell a story: DC-3, DC-6, DC-7, L-188 (Lockheed Electra), B-707, B-720, B-727, B-747. DC-3 to B-747, props to jets, qualifies, I think, as a commercial aviation career. But, of course, there's more to the story.

Chuck was born May 1, 1922 in Eugene, Oregon. He attended the University of Oregon and Oregon State. He entered the Army Air Corps the day after Pearl Harbor was bombed. That's what patriotic young men did in those days. He was trained to fly the B-24 Liberator.

He traveled to Europe via troop ship and there joined the 801st Bomb Group, the "Carpetbaggers." He arrived late in the war (1945) and ended up doing a couple missions dropping "surrender" leaflets. Chuck always joked that he flew his first mission on May 6th and the war ended May 8th. He'd say, "They shoulda sent me over there sooner." Earlier in the war the "Carpetbaggers" flew some serious nighttime missions delivering resistance personnel and supplies behind enemy lines. For those efforts they received a Unit Citation. After the cessation of hostilities, Chuck and his crew flew a B-24 back to the United States. He may have arrived late in the war but his willingness to serve is good enough for me. The Unit Citation and picture of a B-24 now hang in the family room of his oldest son, Tom.

After the war, Chuck flew for Northwest Airlines for thirty-four years, retiring as a B-747 Captain in 1982. His reputation, gleaned from those who knew him, was of a very skilled, true gentleman. He always orchestrated a well run flight, from personal contact with the crew at check-in, to dispatchers, to operations, to mechanics. When all those people like and respect the Captain, the trip *always* goes better. And all liked and respected Chuck Paine.

In retirement, Chuck became an enthusiastic photographer. "Just one more for good measure" was a common refrain heard by his family. Chuck often said, "The two best things I could wish for anybody would be for a great family and a job where you anticipate going to work." Chuck had those things and he was forever grateful.

Then, in 2007, came the beginnings of cognitive decline. Chuck got lost driving from his son's home, in an area where they'd lived for nearly sixty years. The family told BJ, "You can't let Dad drive any more." Chuck said, "I've never had a ticket or an accident." And that was true. But 'tough love' dictated that Chuck no longer drive. BJ bought a different car and Chuck rather accepted it as being "her car" and was content to ride along.

Decline may sometimes seem gradual, but it is also relentless. Chuck would wake up in the night and insist he had to get down to the lobby and "meet up with the crew." BJ, being a long-time airline pilot wife, would then invoke a phrase every airline pilot understands, "Your flight's been cancelled." Chuck accepted that.

None of this is meant to degrade anybody or anything. It's just......life. And I know you understand that.

On Chuck and BJ's 57th wedding anniversary, December 15, 2008, BJ greeted Chuck with, "Good morning, Chuckie boy. Happy Anniversary." Chuck said, "What?" BJ said, "We've been married fifty-seven years today." Chuck replied, "Who told you that?" BJ said, "I've been around the whole fifty-seven, so I know. We married when you were a co-pilot." Chuck answered, "I remember being a co-pilot but I don't remember getting married." That exchange is what the vow "for better or for worse" is about.

Chuck passed away peacefully, with family at his bedside, at a VA Medical Center on January 10, 2009. BJ says, with love, perspective and wisdom, "He had eighty-four very good years out of his eighty-six."

Chuck left a legacy of professionalism that, to this day, is carried on by his family. His oldest son, Tom, is a captain on the MD-11 for Fedex. His youngest son, Randy, flies 757's and 767's for North American Airways, based out of JFK. And Katie, their daughter, called after the US Airways ditching in the Hudson River and said, "Dad would have done that." BJ said, "Done what?" Katie said, "Gone back through the airplane to see if everyone was off."

Both sons gave eulogies at Chuck's memorial. Both mentioned that, as kids, BJ would sometimes take them to the airport (SEATAC) to meet their Dad at the end of a trip. Every time, if he knew they were there, he would flash his landing lights three or four times before pulling into the gate. Then, after shutdown, he would do the same thing with his pen-light from the cockpit. Randy added, "Then my Dad would step onto the jetway and the passengers would thank him for a nice flight and I'd be thinking, 'Wow, my Dad's something special.'" Tom said, "My Dad never smoked or drank and I never heard him use profanity. It was just his personal choice but he was not the least bit judgmental of others. He simply gave us a strong personal foundation to do the right thing." Randy concluded with, "Hey, Dad, you're on takeoff roll now. Set the EPR and just keep on going because you can fly as high as you want now. I miss you and I love you." Tom and Randy spoke for many that day.

Now enter the Blackjack Squadron. The who? The Blackjack Squadron is a group of pilots living in the Seattle, Washington area who fly experimental airplanes-- from Van's RV-series --in formation for their pleasure and for various events and airshows. Many are former military and retired Northwest Airlines pilots. They basically evolved from ·Marty Foy's enjoyment and appreciation of his RV-4's performance, and from his military background. Marty says, "The RV-4 is like flying a little fighter, only much more affordable." Then Wes Schierman acquired a partially completed RV-4, completed it, joined Marty and they had an *element*. Wes was a Northwest Airlines DC-4 co-pilot who was furloughed in 1960. He then volunteered for an active duty tour with the US Air Force. His F-105F was brought down over North Vietnam in 1965 and he was taken POW. He was released in February of 1973. He returned to Northwest Airlines in August of 1973. That tells you a little of his character-- and of the Blackjack Squadron in general. Now numbering some thirty members, many are former military, many are not. But *all* are committed to the training and dedication it takes to fly legitimate formation. And ten were available on February 8, 2009 to fly a missing-man formation for Chuck Paine's memorial service.

The weather on the day of the service was typical Seattle: scuddy. BJ said to them, "I know, as an old airline-pilot-wife, that when push-comes-to-shove, the pilot decides if it's go or no-go." The scud turned out to be high enough and the Blackjack's briefed their formation and a TOT (Time On Target) of 1430 (2:30 PM). It was arranged that the attendees, some two-hundred of them, would be standing outside at that time. In BJ's own words, "We looked up and here they came. Not at 2:28 PM. Not at 2:31 PM. Not even 2:29 PM. But at 2:30 PM." Ten planes together, overhead, until one of them pulled up high and away and flew West-- the Missing Man. Pilots honoring a fellow pilot: the brotherhood. Paul, in attendance, wrote, "BJ had her hand over her heart the whole time."

I never met Chuck Paine. But I know the brotherhood. And I've never met BJ-- Paine with an "i." But I'm glad she wrote me so that I could share this story with you. It's a story of love, family, aviation, the brotherhood....and of life......and remembrance. A remembrance of Chuck Paine's life well lived, now on top of the clouds and in smooth air...forevermore.

48

ALL IN THE FAMILY

Jack built an RV-4. All along, he wanted to keep it in the family. How often does that happen? I don't know, but I understand.

I spent seven years building my RV-8. Someone once said to me, "You're gonna be sad to someday see this thing fly away." I said, "No, I'll never see it fly away. My estate might, but I won't." Point being, it's not exactly easy to think about a personal project/investment of seven years that you've flown and bonded with flying away in the hands of a stranger. At least it isn't for me. Or for Jack. Best to keep it in the family, if at all possible.

Before I tell you the rest of the story, I have to tell you about Jack. You have to know the man to appreciate his passion.

Born in Ashburnham, Massachusetts in 1921, Jack grew up in a red house on Gingerbread Lane. How's that for a setting? Americana. His parents worked hard. His father, a highly skilled toolmaker, was superintendant of The Sawyer Tool Division of T.R.Almond Company; his mother was a homemaker and, with three boys and three girls in the family, was busy. She cooked, sewed, washed, kept ice in the ice box, made root beer and maple syrup, and mended scraped knees and knuckles, not to mention made room for living room boxing matches when Jack's father taught kids how to box. Hard times? From reading her letters, no; she loved it. This was not a home of money and image; this was a home of love and character.

Jack's dad was the Scoutmaster of Troop 18 in Ashburnham for fifty-five years. (Yes, you read that right: *fifty-five* years.) Think he made a difference in the lives of young men? The short answer is, "Yes." The townspeople of Ashburnham named an elementary school after him; it remains to this day.

When Jack graduated from high school, he needed to work and save money for further education. He took a job in a furniture factory for twenty-five cents an hour. Later he took a job that was a step up: twenty-eight cents an hour. But Jack's dad's philosophy always was: "If you learn a trade, you always have a marketable skill." So, in 1940, Jack and his brother Dick enrolled in the Beverly Cooperative Trade School. There they learned all manner of things mechanical.

Jack remembers the night of December 7, 1941. He and his buddy, Don, were listening to music on the radio. The program was interrupted to announce the attack on Pearl Harbor. He and Don were at first puzzled as they tried to visualize where Pearl Harbor was. No matter; they'd know soon enough. The world had just changed and they were about to be swept up in it.

The next day, President Roosevelt declared war on Japan. Military recruiting offices were inundated with young men volunteering for service. Jack was initially deferred from the draft because United Shoe Machine Company, the parent of his trade school, had military contracts. But Jack had always secretly wanted to fly ever since he followed Lindbergh's crossing of the Atlantic. So, one day, he drove to Boston to enlist in the Army Air Corps. He was turned away; they had more applicants than they could process. Down the street was the Naval Aviation Recruiting Station. Before the day was over, Jack was on his way to being inducted. There were many tests and physicals and such until finally, on November 5, 1942, Jack was sworn into the Naval Reserve as an Aviation Cadet….awaiting orders.

On January 6, 1943, Jack's brother Dick was inducted into the Army. (He later went on to fly fifty-five missions in B-25s over Europe.) On February 8, 1943, Jack's orders arrived. He was to report for active duty. These were exciting times for young men, emotional times for parents. Jack's father once spent a day in bed, wrought with grief.

Jack reported for duty in Keene, New Hampshire, only thirty miles from his home, and flew his first dual flight February 12, 1943, flying a J-3 Cub on skis. He soloed ten days later, on February 22nd. The world was at war; there was no time to be wasted. But something else was happening, too. The hook was set: flying was to be a part of Jack's life now and forevermore.

Jack was next sent to Olathe, Kansas to train in the N2S (Stearman). From there it was on to Pensacola, Florida to fly the Vultee Valiant, also known as the "Vultee Vibrator," or SNV. And then he was selected to fly the SNJ (Army Air Corps designation: AT-6).

The SNJ was an airplane that Jack grew to love. Perhaps partially for that reason, after he received his Navy wings, he was selected to be a flight instructor in the SNJ. And that's what he did and where he was when, in 1945 in the Officer's Club, he heard over the radio, "The war is over!!"

Jack came home and tried, as did many, to make a living flying airplanes. It worked for awhile, but not for long. He married Margaret (Peg). She remembers him walking through the office and thinking to herself, "Oooohhh, he's cute." Well, "he's cute" turned into fifty-six years of marriage and counting. Together they raised four boys and two girls. And Jack worked for Sears Roebuck for thirty-four years to make a living for his family. But the love of flight always lingered in his heart. Always.

Now you know something of the background and character of the man.

Then it happened: Jack discovered airplane homebuilding. He discovered it the same way a lot of us have: saw a picture, read an ad, took a demo ride and….done deal! His heart now had a place for his hands to go. He started building his RV-4 in 1985. He finished in 1992. For five years it was in the basement of his home; for two years it was in the garage. It was then taken to the airport for final assembly. First flight was May 28, 1992. Jack was back, full circle: from reading about Lindbergh, to Naval Aviator, to marriage, family and work, and back to flying. Is his airplane special to him? Safely, the answer is "yes." Would he ever want to see a stranger fly it away? I think not. Jack's airplane is a part of his soul.

Jack happily flew his airplane for thirteen years. Aloft, he was once again the person he was always happiest being: a pilot.

Then, as happens in life, the hammer fell. Jack lost his medical. He fought it for awhile; there were questions. But, quite often, once the Feds get going down a track it's very difficult to turn the train around. It hit him hard. He didn't even want to go to the hangar. Eventually he found some peace and would go visit his old friend. But there was strain: talkin' to it isn't the same as flyin' it.

Now the plot thickens. Jack had soloed his son Mike in a J-3 some twenty-five years ago. But Mike has been busy doing other things, like making a living and raising a family. He remains, however, the one offspring with a lingering aviation interest. Mike and his bride, Susie, have two children, daughter Lauren and son Zack. Lauren met Jerome while attending Auburn, where Jerome, an up and coming young pilot, was enrolled in the aviation program. They became girlfriend/boyfriend. Jerome jumped through all the aviation hoops and was hired by a regional airline. And then-- a sign of the times, I suppose --was furloughed in pretty short order. But, to his credit, he's still chasing the dream. Among other things, he got his tail wheel endorsement.

Now guess who's coming to Jack's hometown? The guru of all things RV and all around good guy, Mike Seager. Jack gets to thinking and calls son Mike and asks if he'd like to come up from his home in Georgia to Jack's home in Cicero, New York for some RV dual with Mr. Seager. Jack then sweetened the deal with a promise of some of Peg's apple pie. Mike got to thinking....'Jerome's more current than I and just got his tail wheel endorsement.' They both agree to come. That called for yet another apple pie.

With all this in mind, Jack got his good friend and master mechanic, Bernie, to help him look over the airplane. They went over it with a fine tooth comb and signed off the annual.

Then Mike and Jerome arrived. Both took some RV dual from Mr. Seager. Then Jerome climbed into the RV-4 and Jack familiarized him with the cockpit. Jerome started the airplane, spent about ten minutes taxiing about and.....then.....took off. Now to get it back on the ground.

Jack said, "I wasn't worried. Jerome's very thorough, very professional. He's just a fine young man." Jack was right. Jerome flew around for about thirty-minutes and then made a fine landing. On engine shutdown, when Jerome opened the canopy, Jack was one of the first to greet him. He asked, "Did I oversell it?" Jerome said, "No." And then added, "You wear this airplane."

Jack sent me an e-mail that evening: "Wanted you to be one of the first to know that Jerome had the Four up for a half hour today and there is peculiar distortion to his countenance."

Before they left the hangar that day, Jack walked over to his airplane and said to Jerome, "Put your hand on the cowling. It's warm again!" Jerome didn't have to put his hand on the cowling. It was Jack's heart that was warm.

Jack is giving RV-4 N918RB to Mike and he and Lauren and Jerome can work out the details. Details aside, Jack's airplane, and Jack's passion, stays in the family. And, as they say in all fairy tail endings, lives happily ever after.

49

FLYING FOR FUN

I recently finished recurrent ground school at my airline. It was magnificent. We discussed GCU's, BBPU's, DC GEN's, AC GENS's, TRU's, PSEU's, ECU's, FIBAR, LOGGERS and WOW lights. We even got into ZNTOL, DDTOL, and "six-six-and-six." And spoilers, TCAS, GPW and TCA's. I even passed the test!

Well, I did miss some of the "Chakerian Questions." (Chakerian's the guy who updated the test.) You know the type questions I'm talking about:

"What is the square root of the fuel output of the HMU at takeoff power? Consider the coefficient of expansion for titanium at ISA +20 in your answer and show your work."

There was one thing that was *not* mentioned during the three days of ground school: ***flying for fun.***

Yeah, just flying for fun-- the reason most of us got started in this aviation business. In all our modern day sophistication I think the concept of *fun* often gets overlooked. Sure, professional aviation is a serious business, but it's not so serious that we shouldn't occasionally rekindle the spirit of flying just for the joy of it.

So when I got home I put on my jeans, cowboy boots and my "Real Airplanes Have Round Engines" t-shirt and sauntered out to the local aerodrome. Opened the hangar door and there it sat. Stearman. Fifty years old, sitting on its tail, nose pointed proudly up. No cockpit key. No cockpit door. No cockpit roof.

Walked around it. Patted it. Fine linen. Talked to it. Asked it how it was doing. Checked the oil. Got some on me and wiped it on my pants.

The fun was beginning.

Pushed it out into the sunshine. Looked at it. Pure. Simple. Strong. The heart beats a little faster; the soul comes alive.

Got in. Seat belt on, just like an airliner. Similarity stops there, however. Flight controls are manual: no hydraulics, no spoilers. You check the connections by looking down beneath your feet. No floor, just a couple of boards where your feet go. Before you go and get uppity on me, the Stearman *does* have hydraulics: the brakes. You tap the pedals and a rod goes into a cylinder that has a line that goes to the wheels and expands some stuff in there. 'Bout all you need to know-- don't use 'em much anyway. Anti-skid? Anti-skid is a ground loop. We try not to use anti-skid.

Fuel system? You bet. We have one. No electronic enrichment, however. Throttle is connected to a rod that disappears through a firewall and goes to....get this...a c a r b u r e t o r. I know it's there because I bolted it on. Didn't use any metric tools either.

Fuel quantity system? Yup. Cork floats in the gas. Cork has a wire on it that I can see through a sight gauge. Single point refuel, too. Only one fuel cap.

Switch on! It's the shiny one. I emphasize "one" because it is about the *only* one. Kinda clicks when you turn it on. They tell me that click is the solenoid. Doesn't matter. If it doesn't click, it doesn't work.

Thumb on the button we found on one of the dusty hangar shelves and the prop turns. The engine sputters, coughs and starts. Eventually all the clanking stops and the round engine settles into idle. Smoke. Vibration. Wind in the face. Words can't describe......

"Taxi to 10L via Sierra Six to Bravo, then Sierra Five to the inner ramp, then Echo Two to Echo?" Nope. Just mosey over to where the grass is mashed down. Don't get uppity on me again. We *have* a radio. Just can't hear it very well over all the beautiful engine sounds. It detracts. We know when we have to use it. Don't have to use it to mosey.

Center line lights? Transmissometers? CAT II hold lines? Sorry. Center line weeds, maybe. Line up on the weeds. Push the throttle forward. Autofeather? Hope not. Only have one feather. Tail comes up. How many airliners can do that? The runway that was hidden behind the engine appears. Then disappears. Couple hundred feet to flight. Again, how many airliners can do that? Gear up? Nope. They are welded where they need to be. Leave them alone, thank you very much. Flaps up? Not!

"Contact departure control?" Sure. Wave to the small crowd that generally gathers when the Stearman flies. Don't put your arm too far into the slipstream, though. You're going darn near ninety. Your arm will involuntarily conform to the slipstream if you're not careful.

VOR? Transponder? Radar vectors? RNAV? GPS? MLS? Naw, just roads, rivers, towns and mountains.

Settle in. Noise. Wind. Slow moving scenery. Guy on the combine disappears beneath the leading edge of the lower wing. He reappears shortly thereafter beneath the trailing edge. Guy in the boat on the river makes a u-turn and stops. I watch the wake dissipate. I look up. Blue sky. My goggles just about blow off my face. This is flying; this is fun. It just doesn't get any better'n this. It just doesn't. I fly on to make it last. I am lost in joy....

Return for landing. Vectors to the localizer and couple-up the autopilot? Right! Line up on final. Runway disappears behind the round engine up front. Pick out some landmarks at the end of the runway I know are there. Grass rushes by under the lower wing. Wheels touch and I begin talking sternly to my airplane, "Go straight. Go straight. Go straight. Don't you even try to swap ends." It goes straight. I don't have to use the anti-skid.

Taxi to the hangar. Don't have to use the hydraulic system (the brakes, remember?). Just throttle on back and she comes to a stop. Shut her down. Don't move. Just sit there. Listen. Light breeze. Engine crackles. Reflect: This is living. The world would be a better place if more people could experience this. It really would.

Push her back in the hangar; gotta go fly the airliner tomorrow. Sophistication. Weather. Traffic. Don't get me wrong; I love what I do. I know it would be difficult for an airline to show a profit with a fleet of Stearmans. But no where in the operations manuals, the standards manuals or the FAR's does the word "fun" appear. When is the last time you heard the FAA use that word? So I just went out and made it so. You can, too. All you need is a small airplane-- I prefer fabric and tailwheels, but I certainly won't begrudge you metal with a nosewheel --to fly off a small airport far from a city on a nice day. It's where it's at! I promise.

Back to airline ground school instructor/friend Chakerian. Remember? The square root guy? I think I can lead him to the truth. In fact, I know I can because he said he'd buy the gas. I have him studying for *my* ground school. I'm gonna ask him, "How many wings does a Stearman have?"

Answer: enough to fly for the fun of it.

5820392R0

Made in the USA
Charleston, SC
07 August 2010